Cambridge Opera Handbooks

C. W. von Gluck
Orfeo

Act II of *Orpheus und Eurydike*, Staatsoper, Munich,
March 1953. Producer, Wieland Wagner

C. W. von Gluck
Orfeo

Compiled by
PATRICIA HOWARD
Lecturer in music
The Open University

CAMBRIDGE UNIVERSITY PRESS

Cambridge
London   New York   New Rochelle
Melbourne   Sydney

Published by the Press Syndicate of the University of Cambridge
The Pitt Building, Trumpington Street, Cambridge CB2 1RP
32 East 57th Street, New York, NY 10022, USA
296 Beaconsfield Parade, Middle Park, Melbourne 3206, Australia

First published 1981

Printed in Great Britain
at the University Press, Cambridge

British Library Cataloguing in Publication Data

Howard, Patricia, b. 1937
C. W. von Gluck, Orfeo – (Cambridge opera handbooks).
1. Gluck, Christoph Willibald, Ritter von. Orfeo
I. Title   II. Series
782. 1'092'4   M410.G5   80-49734

ISBN 0 521 22827 1 hard covers
ISBN 0 521 29664 1 paperback

CAMBRIDGE OPERA HANDBOOKS

General preface

This is a series of studies of individual operas, written for the serious opera-goer or record-collector as well as the student or scholar. Each volume has three main concerns. The first is historical: to describe the genesis of the work, its sources or its relation to literary prototypes, the collaboration between librettist and composer, and the first performance and subsequent stage history. This history is itself a record of changing attitudes towards the work, and an index of general changes of taste. The second is analytical and is grounded in a very full synopsis which considers the opera as a structure of musical and dramatic effects. In most volumes there is also a musical analysis of a section of the score, showing how the music serves or makes the drama. The analysis, like the history, naturally raises questions of interpretation, and the third concern of each volume is to show how critical writing about an opera, like production and performance, can direct or distort appreciation of its structural elements. Some conflict of interpretation is an inevitable part of this account; editors of the handbooks reflect this – by citing classic statements, by commissioning new essays, by taking up their own critical position. A final section gives a select bibliography, a discography and guides to other sources.

In working out plans for these volumes, the Cambridge University Press was responding to an initial stimulus from staff of the English National Opera. Particular thanks are due to Mr Edmund Tracey and Mr Nicholas John for help, advice and suggestions.

Books Published

Richard Wagner: *Parsifal* by Lucy Beckett
W. A. Mozart: *Don Giovanni* by Julian Rushton

Other volumes in preparation

Contents

Illustrations

Acknowledgements

This book stands as a tribute to the work of many Gluck scholars of the
past. In particular, I welcome the opportunity to record my debt to the
painstaking factual research of Lionel de la Laurencie and Alfred
Loewenberg and the inspiring perception and understanding of Romain
Rolland. I should like to express my warmest gratitude to all who have
worked with me on this volume: to my co-writers, Eve Barsham, John
Eliot Gardiner, Tom Hammond, Hans Heimler, Sir Charles Mackerras,
Kevin Smith and Malcolm Walker; and to many librarians, especially
Magnus John of the Open University Library and representatives of the
British Library, the Bibliothèque Nationale, Paris, and the Stadt- und
Landesbibliothek and the Staatsarchiv, Vienna

1 The Orpheus myth in operatic history

BY EVE BARSHAM

Mythical stories of a mortal reclaimed from the kingdom of the dead are common to the cultures of both East and West. They may take the form of a man rescuing a woman (wife or sister) or even, as in the Hindu story of Savitri and Satyavan, of a woman pleading for the return to life of her spouse. As in the last-named, some versions of the myth have a happy ending, but for Eurydice in the Orpheus story there is only a second, irreversible death. This story, referred to in Greek literature as early as the seventh century B.C., and subsequently retold, briefly or at length, by poets and dramatists as far removed in time as Ovid, Virgil, Pindar, Shakespeare, Milton, Pope, Rilke, Valéry and Cocteau, has attracted composers of lyric drama from the emergence of the art form in the late fifteenth century until modern times.

The legend varies in certain details from one source to another. The outlines of the story as narrated by Virgil in the *Georgics* Book IV (written about 35 B.C.) are as follows. Eurydice, the wife of the singer Orpheus, has been bitten by a snake whilst escaping from the unwelcome attentions of a suitor. She dies, and Orpheus follows her, mourning, into the underworld, where Proserpine authorises her release on condition that Orpheus does not look back at her until they have regained the earth. Near the end of their journey, Orpheus, in a moment of passion and folly, looks back, thus violating the condition. Eurydice, who had not provoked this backward glance, reproaches him bitterly as she returns irrevocably to Hades. For months Orpheus weeps as he plays his lyre, surrounded by the trees and animals drawn by the sound of his music. The Circonian women, insulted by his mourning in the midst of their Bacchanalian rites, tear him to pieces. The river Hebrus receives his dismembered body and, as the head travels downstream, his voice can be heard calling the name of Eurydice while the banks echo the dying sounds.

Ovid's account in the *Metamorphoses* Books X-XI was written about forty years after Virgil's narrative, and differs from it in Eurydice's

1

reaction to Orpheus's unprovoked turning to look back at her. He is fearful that she might fail him during the silent climb upwards to earth from Hades, but it is he who fails. When he turns to her, she does not reproach him, but dies, uttering one last farewell. Orpheus prays to be allowed to cross the river Styx a second time and descend once again to the underworld, but the ferryman Charon drives him back. After a period of mourning, he suffers a violent death at the hands of the Thracian women, and his shade flees to the underworld where he is reunited with Eurydice.

It is easy to understand why this story of the power of love and of music against the inevitability of human weakness and of death should have appealed to the early poets and composers of lyric drama. Opera evolved as an indirect result of the revival of secular drama which was one of the glories of the renaissance in fifteenth-century Italy. Many new plays were written, in Latin or in the vernacular, modelled on classical dramas, for performance at Italian courts. Most comedies included music, such as solos, choruses and instrumental pieces, at the beginning or end of an act, and between the acts a musical entertainment based on a myth or allegory might be presented. Such an interlude was called an *intermedio,* and could, on special occasions of celebration, be quite extensive in scope. Incidental music also accompanied the many *pastorali* that were written from the middle of the fifteenth century onwards. A *pastorale* was a play featuring the gentle amorous exploits of shepherds and shepherdesses against a rural background, the setting and the quality of the language, rather than the plot, forming the main interest. An early writer of such *pastorali* was Angelo Poliziano, whose *Orfeo,* a poem of 434 lines, was written in the space of two days, and partly set to music possibly by Germi, a composer of whom nothing more is known. The work was performed at Mantua, probably on 18 July 1472. The poet, a protégé of Lorenzo the Magnificent, was then only seventeen years of age. Although the music has not survived, the drama was published in 1494 at Bologna and is described by Charles Burney in his *General History* (II, p. 507). There are five acts, in the first of which, described as 'pastorale', the song of Aristeo, the rival to Orpheus, is the main feature. In the second act, 'ninfale', a chorus of Dryads laments Eurydice's death — she was bitten by a serpent while fleeing from Aristeo. Act III, 'eroico', seems to have been sung throughout: it consists of some 'heroic' stanzas for Orpheus and the recounting of Eurydice's death by a Dryad. Orpheus descends to the infernal regions in the fourth act, 'nigromantico', where he encounters Pluto, Proserpine, Eurydice and Tesiphon. Eurydice is released on the usual condition, which is inevitably broken. In the last act, 'baccanale', Orpheus is destroyed by the Maenads. Poliziano's text was set to music again by Pietro della Viola in 1486, and surely influenced the Florentine poet, Ottavio Rinuccini, who wrote the libretto for the earliest extant operas, Peri's and Caccini's settings of *L'Euridice*, in 1600.

Meanwhile, since the mid fifteenth century, the interest in classical culture was further manifested in the gathering together of noblemen and scholars in Rome, Milan, Mantua and other Italian cities into 'academies' — groups within which philosophy and various branches of science and the arts could be discussed and ideas exchanged. These societies were known by such distinctive names as the Filarmonici, the Arcadi, the Filomusi and so on, and a special bias towards music was a feature of the Camerata in Florence where, during the fifteenth century, Lorenzo the Magnificent had created a wide circle of culture in which musicians could find a place. The results of the exchanges of the Florentine Camerata, which met at the house of one Count Bardi, during the latter half of the sixteenth century, were far-reaching. Among the earlier members of this group were Vincenzo Galilei, a competent composer and father of the famous astronomer, and a Roman theoretician, Girolamo Mei, who seems to have initiated the attempt to imitate ancient Greek solo song, in so far as the then available evidence in Greek literature made it possible to speculate on its nature. The name given to this new type of vocal line was monody. It consisted of declamation in free rhythm, rather akin to sung speech, following the natural inflection of the words. The accompaniment to this was a single chordal one, as might have been strummed on the lyre (though there was some confusion among these Florentine amateurs between the simple ancient harp-like instrument, and the fifteenth-century *lyra da gamba* which was played with a bow). Galilei, who had begun by composing polyphonic madrigals, published in Florence in 1581 a *Dialogue about Ancient and Modern Music* in which he renounced and severely criticised contrapuntal technique on the grounds that the clarity of the words was lost in the chaos of varied rhythms and movement of parts. Word painting (common in madrigals), he contended, should give place to a supple melodic line which would increase the intensity of the poetry. The relevance for these early experimenters of the mythological character of Orpheus, with his expressive yet simply delivered and accompanied song, can be seen to be overwhelming.

Galilei's own attempts at monody are no longer extant. Undoubtedly they would strike a modern listener as austere, but the extremism of his theories was modified by two members of a new generation of the

Camerata, the composers Jacopo Peri and Giulio Caccini. These, being professional singers, realised that the restrictive nature of Galilei's type of melodic line would inhibit both singer and composer. Caccini's own monodic songs with lute accompaniment, written in the 1590s, use a certain amount of ornamentation while keeping the inflections of the words clear, and these, together with an explanatory preface, were published in Florence in 1602 under the title *Le nuove musiche.*

The 'coincidence' of the beginning of opera was near at hand, and the role of the new opera composers closely mirrored that of the mythical Orpheus, as they struggled to express every vestige of the text at hand. The new type of melodic line was nowhere more suitable for use than in settings of dramatic verse. And within the long-established tradition of the *intermedio* and of incidental music to plays such as *pastorali,* the Orpheus story offered a peculiarly appropriate plot (it was set by, for example, Zarlino in 1574 and Visconti in 1599). The new genre of opera sprang from the association of a poet and a composer both in sympathy with the new style: two members of the Camerata, the poet Rinuccini and the singer-composer Peri, first collaborated in writing the opera *Dafne,* produced with great acclaim in 1597. The success of this opera, or *dramma per musica* as it was termed, of which only the libretto has survived, led to the commission of a new work by Peri and Rinuccini to celebrate the marriage of Henry IV of France to Maria de' Medici, and thus *L'Euridice,* the first extant opera, was performed at the Pitti Palace in Florence on 6 October 1600.

In fact the music was partly the work of Caccini, and each composer published a separate setting of the same libretto in the following year; the reader may gather from the prefaces to each score that there was no little rivalry in the situation. Caccini's setting, though it reached publication a few weeks before Peri's, nevertheless had to wait until 1602 for a much less spectacular première, and he appears to have received no more remuneration for his work than a good dinner!

The style of the Peri-Caccini setting of *L'Euridice* was termed *stile rappresentativo* (theatre style). It consisted mainly of recitative over a bass, the effect being of a compromise between song and speech. There are a few strophic arias and homophonic choruses for dancing, but very little polyphonic writing. Rinuccini's pastoral poem, which takes about ninety minutes in performance, begins with a narration by a messenger (sung by a boy treble) of Eurydice's death. Then follows Orpheus's lament, and a mourning chorus. In the next scene, entitled 'Epiphany', Arcetro, a friend of Orpheus, describes the descent of Venus from heaven to comfort Orpheus and to encourage him to rescue Eurydice from the underworld. The following scene, 'Descent into hell', begins with a dialogue between Orpheus and Venus, and continues with a solo by Orpheus before he pleads with Pluto. The scene ends with a solemn chorus of Shades. Finally, in 'Resurrection', a messenger announces the joyful return of Orpheus and Eurydice. No condition had been attached to the rescue of the heroine, so the story is devoid of conflict or tragedy. Orpheus sings a solo and the work ends with choruses and dances.

This opera – which was revived in Naples in 1920, in Florence in 1923 and in Munich in 1934 – made an enormous impact on its distinguished audience in 1600, not only because of the interpretative skill of the singers (Peri himself took the role of Orpheus) but also because of the novelty of the style and the feeling that here was an authentic replica of classical Greek drama. And yet without a composer of genius to follow on, this new art form might have proved to be merely a phenomenon of passing interest, since something more than musical competence and a set of theories, however rational, is needed to start a living tradition. Among the audience in Florence had been the composer Claudio Monteverdi, and it was his own first attempt at opera, *La favola d'Orfeo,* performed semi-privately at the Accademia degl'Invaghiti at Mantua during the Carnival of 1607, which at a stroke lifted the new form onto the highest artistic plane.

Though the starting-point for Monteverdi's style of recitative is the monodic *stile rappresentativo* of Peri and Caccini, yet his recitative has more formal organisation. Some ornamentation is used, and at one point in the score (published in 1609) is written out on an extra stave, thus providing an object-lesson in the conventions of embellishment employed at this time. In addition to the recitatives, which are often melodic in character, solo arias, dances and choruses in polyphonic, madrigalian style provide the variety lacking in the operas of 1600, which have virtually nothing like contrapuntal writing. Above all, the highly expressive character of the music – its portrayal of a variety of emotions, and the richness and diversity of the writing – prove conclusively that in the composer's mind it was no longer subservient to the words, as Galilei (and later Calzabigi) insisted it should be. Indeed, the parallels between the composers of early opera and Orpheus himself are continually jostling for acknowledgement: the expressive power of Monteverdi's music triumphed in Mantua just as Orpheus's music tamed Charon at the entrance to the underworld. Monteverdi's orchestra of about forty players, comprising woodwind, brass, string and continuo instruments, represents a kind of summary of sixteenth-century ensembles – a large force compared with the harpsichord, theorbo, *lira grande* and lute which accompanied Peri's opera, and in fact larger than any opera orchestra for at least the next hundred years.

The poet of *La favola d'Orfeo* was himself an instrumentalist and the son of a composer. Alessandro Striggio was chancellor to the Mantuan court, and had been in close contact with the Florentine Camerata since his father had been in the service of the Medicis in Florence during the 1560s. Inspired by the sixteenth-century poet Tasso, his drama of Orpheus is divided into five acts, and was originally devised as a tragedy following the outlines of Virgil's and Ovid's narratives, ending with the violent death of Orpheus at the hands of the jealous Thracian women. But Monteverdi modified the last act so that the despair of Orpheus is tempered with consolation. Act I consists of rejoicing over the marriage of Orpheus and Eurydice. In Act II, after a song for the shepherds, Orpheus himself sings, only to be interrupted by a messenger bringing news of Eurydice's death. Orpheus cries 'Tu sei morta' ('Thou art dead') and a chorus of shepherds concludes the act with a lament. In Act III Orpheus attempts to gain entrance to Hades, singing a song of testing quality. Charon allows him to pass, and in Act IV Orpheus's plea for Eurydice's release is debated by Pluto and Proserpine. On the usual condition, he is permitted to lead her back to earth, but in the midst of a joyful song, he looks back to see if she is following. The Shades lament the new catastrophe. Act V shows Orpheus mourning on the plains of Thrace, until his father Apollo descends to take him up to heaven where, among the stars, he will be reunited with his bride. This provides the opportunity for a spectacular machine-effect, and the apotheosis gives the drama a happy resolution.

Monteverdi's was the third setting of the Orpheus story to achieve historical significance. Within the next dozen years two more settings of the story, *Orfeo dolente* (1616) by Domenico Belli and *La morte d'Orfeo* (1619), a pastoral tragi-comedy by Stefano Landi, were performed in Florence and Rome respectively. It is an indication of their significance and success that both were published immediately. Landi, incidentally, was the first composer to write his own libretto, so the traditional contest for supremacy between words and music was on this occasion suspended.

Nearly thirty years were to pass before another important setting of the Orpheus story was staged. This was Luigi Rossi's *L'Orfeo*, commissioned by Cardinal Mazarin for performance at the Palais Cardinal in Paris in 1647. Many changes had taken place in the intervening decades, and some may be accounted for by the fact that since 1637, when the first public opera house opened in Venice, opera audiences were no longer composed exclusively of cultured aristocrats. The underlying ideology of the art form was fast being forgotten, and an entertainment in which music and spectacle were the predominant considerations was taking its place. The plot in Rossi's lengthy opera is complicated, with a large cast and many spectacular scenes engineered by the machinist Torelli. There are even comic episodes, unthinkable in the early operatic versions of the story. Set to a tedious libretto by Buti, the recitatives are the least interesting part of the music, but the beauty of the arias, and the quality of melancholy lyricism which the French admired so much, more than atoned for the disappointing lack of real drama in the piece. It enjoyed a huge success despite the criticisms of objectors who protested at expenditure on such luxurious entertainments while the people starved.

The French had earlier assimilated the ideas generated by the Florentine Camerata about music and poetry, and had evolved a theatrical entertainment – the court ballet – in which music, poetry and dance were combined. But their love of dancing resulted in the overshadowing of poetry by the two other elements, and this characteristic national approach was to influence opera in France right through the eighteenth century. It created the conditions which prompted Gluck to rewrite his original Italianate score of *Orfeo* to suit the French national traditions – a rewriting which will be examined later in this volume.

Space does not permit a detailed description of the many Orpheus operas which appeared after the middle of the seventeenth century, nor could a list be complete. Composers seem to have been attracted to this particular myth by the implied message about the power of music which it contains, by the spiritual conflict portrayed in the return from Hades, and also by the pastoral setting of its early scenes, and the opportunities for bizarre effects (spectacular settings, dances of Furies and Blessed Spirits) in the underworld episode. Among the composers who chose the Orpheus story are Loewe (1659), Sartorio (1672), Keiser (1698), Hasse (with others, 1736), J. C. Bach (a version of Gluck's score, 1770), Bertoni (a setting of Calzabigi's libretto, 1776), Naumann (partly based on Calzabigi, 1786), Haydn (1791), Krenek (1926), Milhaud (1926) and Casella (1932).

Calzabigi's selection of this myth for his libretto, which he then (by his own account) 'chose Gluck' to compose, may well have reflected a wish to return to the first principles of the Florentine Camerata. The original 1762 version of Gluck's and Calzabigi's *Orfeo* takes about ninety minutes in performance, the same length of time as Peri's setting. In contrast to the large cast in, for instance, Rossi's *Orfeo* or Haydn's

L'anima del filosofo – in which latter, besides the chief characters, there are parents, confidants, deities of the underworld and other solo singing parts – the reduction in the number of protagonists to three has the effect of concentrating the spectator's attention on the central conflict. Nor are there any sub-plots to provide light relief, or to weaken the progress of the drama, and this 'unity' of the action is reminiscent of the conventions of Greek tragedy. Calzabigi may be said to have observed the other Greek unities as well: by setting the scene of Eurydice's burial-place by the lake of Averno, near to the entrance of the underworld, he has, as he says in the preface to the 1764 score, preserved the unity of place; and by compressing the events to the duration of one day and one night, he has maintained the unity of time.

Clearly Calzabigi had read the accounts of the story as narrated by Virgil and Ovid, though his reference to sources in the 1764 preface does not actually include a mention of the latter poet at all (an omission rectified by Gluck later in his own preface to the 1774 score). Calzabigi's unsigned *argomento* (an 'argument' being a description of the scene and plot of a play) begins with a two-line quotation from Virgil's *Georgics* Book IV, which may be translated,

> He sang of thee, sweet wife, of thee on the lonely shore,
> Of thee at daybreak and at nightfall.

The poet goes on to outline the plot very briefly, remarking that 'in order to adapt the story to the stage, I have had to modify the tragic ending'. Calzabigi's modifications begin during the scene of the return to earth after Eurydice has been released from the underworld. According to both Virgil and Ovid, the blame for Orpheus's fatal backward glance lies solely with him, the result of his doubt and reckless passion. But Calzabigi transfers the feeling of mistrust to Eurydice, causing her to provoke Orpheus; and since she was not allowed to be aware of the condition for her release, imposed in this version by Cupid, her protestations and bewilderment seem convincing and justified. This situation also generates more external drama and interplay of reactions than could an inner turmoil undergone by Orpheus alone, leading an unprotesting spouse back to earth. The *deus ex machina* happy ending, which often strikes a modern audience as illogical and unnecessary, was a common and accepted convention in neoclassical drama, whose audiences were troubled at the moral implications of undeserved suffering. For Gluck and Calzabigi – and for their audiences – it did not seriously invalidate or weaken the preceding drama.

And so Calzabigi writes the minimum of words, selects only the central events of the story and uses the smallest possible number of characters. Moreover, he seems to anticipate Wagner's reason, eighty years later, for the choice of mythical subjects on which to base his own libretti, namely that a mythical story is eternally true. It is more concentrated, intense and significant than any other type of plot, and hence there is a timeless, continually relevant quality about the character of Orpheus. Unlike the characters in, for instance, the later operas of Verdi, who are portrayed in depth and develop as human beings during the course of the opera, the character of Orpheus, around whom the whole action revolves, is static. It does not progress as the story unfolds. Orpheus was always a symbolic figure. From the earliest representations in opera, it was clear that he 'stood for' the power of art, and especially music. Incidents in the story which showed him visibly and audibly charming Charon, or the gods of the underworld, or the Furies, by the brilliance or beauty of his song, gave the composer an opportunity to produce music which made that power audible. Inevitably, this provoked further reflection on the relative status of words and music. It is no accident that Orpheus was claimed as a kind of patron saint by both renaissance poets and the opera-composers of the baroque. Inevitably the musicians claimed that their art was the more powerful, and opera was a chance to demonstrate it.

The legendary singer became a kind of magus. The union of almost magical art and almost superhuman fidelity is reflected in the strength and austerity of Gluck's music, to produce a truly classical lyric drama on the subject of the apotheosis of song.

But, deliberately backward-looking as Gluck's opera is in many ways, paradoxically it was the most forward-looking opera of its time, and the starting-point for many of the new developments in opera during the next century. Once again, the Orpheus myth had made history.

2 The libretto

BY PATRICIA HOWARD

The grand coincidence of the reform

Gluck's 'reform of opera' is often presented as the work of one man: a single-handed enterprise which changed the whole course of operatic history. Candidates for the position of the one man vary. Gluck himself is only rarely named; the librettist Calzabigi is the favourite. But the opera's promoter Durazzo, its choreographer Angiolini, the designer Quaglio and even the universally influential Rousseau are often highlighted for the role of prime mover.

The truth is that neither one nor all of these can be called the chief instigators of the reform. *Orfeo* came into being because of a much larger series of coincidences. It is the product of its age. Not only did the passing fashions of the mid-eighteenth-century theatre, with its penchant for verisimilitude in acting and decor, play their part in shaping Gluck's opera, but the touchstone of the age of enlightenment, the value placed on the sincere expression of simple human emotions, is everywhere apparent in the opera, making it in every sense a child of its time. Theatrical fashions did no more than reflect this value. The search after realism and nature was widespread in the theatre: the expressive mime of Garrick in London, the new 'danza parlante' ('eloquent dance') of Angiolini in Vienna, and the simple and sensationally revealing costumes of his rival Noverre in Berlin, Stuttgart and Lyons, are indicative of the extent of the spirit of experimentation and the scope of its application.

Gluck probably first encountered this spirit when he came to London in 1745. He himself told Charles Burney in 1772 that 'he owed entirely to England the study of nature in his dramatic compositions'. Coming to England 'at a very disadvantageous period [when] Handel was then so high in fame, that no one would willingly listen to any other than to his compositions', Gluck claimed to have

studied the English taste; remarked particularly what the audience seemed most to feel; and finding that plainness and simplicity had the greatest effect upon them, he has, ever since that time, endeavoured to write for the voice, more in the natural tones of the human affections

10

and passions, than to flatter the lovers of deep science or difficult execution; and it may be remarked, that most of his airs in *Orfeo* are as plain and simple as English ballads.

(Burney, *Music in Germany*, p. 92)

This surprising statement may have been no more than a polite compliment to the English scholar Gluck was addressing. Supposing it to be his genuine analysis of the roots of his innovatory simplicity of style, however, we need to know what influence from his brief London visit had so profound and lasting an effect: seventeen years were to elapse between the visit and the composition of *Orfeo*.

We know that on this occasion Gluck met Handel and that he venerated him for the remainder of his life. A portrait of Handel hung in his bedroom and Gluck used to declare: 'There is the portrait of the most inspired master of our art; when I open my eyes in the morning I look upon him with reverential awe, and acknowledge him as such' (quoted in Kelly, *Reminiscences,* p. 255). And it was Handel who advised Gluck to take less trouble for English audiences – an obscure remark in view of the fact that the operas Gluck put on in London were all pastiches, largely cobbled together from earlier works. Moreover, Handel's decidedly pragmatic advice seems unlikely to have given rise to the noble simplicity of Gluck's mature works.

Another possible influence on Gluck at this time is that of the actor David Garrick. Garrick's impact on the spoken theatre corresponded closely to Gluck's on opera, and was effected twenty years earlier. Before Garrick and Gluck, the traditions of tragedy and *opera seria* were similar in terms of stage effect. In both genres, one character at a time would dominate the stage, holding a fixed and statuesque gesture while declaiming a speech or singing an aria. The presentation of one emotion at a time betrays the out-dated aesthetic governing this acting style: the connection is clear between this tradition of one speech/one gesture, and the convention of one movement/one emotion in late baroque music.

But Garrick's reform, and later Gluck's, changed all this. Garrick's admirers dwelt both on his range of dramatic expression and on its realism: 'His face expresses all the passions one after the other, and that without any grimace' (Collé, *Journal,* 13 July 1751, quoted in Hedgcock, *David Garrick,* p. 109). His skill in mime was widely praised. It was noticed that he continued to act during the speeches of others without 'either looking contemptibly on an inferior performer, unnecessarily spitting, or suffering his eyes to wander through the whole circle of spectators' (quoted in Heartz, 'From Garrick to Gluck', p. 112). His eloquence particularly attracted foreign observers. The choreographer Noverre wrote of him: 'He was so natural and so true to life, his gestures and facial expressions were so eloquent and persuasive, that he enabled even those who understood not a word of English to follow the action' (Noverre, *Lettres*, IX). It is significant that reports of Gluck's operas in performance often drew similar language from the critics:

Monsieur Le Gros [who created the role of Orpheus in the Paris production of 1774] animated and, dare we say inspired by the composer, rose to the occasion and augmented the magic of his role with acting full of feeling, eloquence and pathos. It was not only as a singer that he was admirable, but as a true-to-life actor, full of passion.

(*Mercure de France,* October 1774, p. 167)

Gluck came into contact with Garrick's art twice in his lifetime. During much of that brief London visit, when Gluck claimed to have first realised the dramatic potential of the 'natural tones of the human affections and passions', Garrick was in Dublin. But it seems probable that Gluck was still in London, directing the opera at the King's Theatre, when Garrick returned. And if so, Gluck would have had the chance of seeing the great actor play five Shakespearean roles in less than three weeks. Gluck subsequently made closer contact, if not with Garrick, then with one of his pupils: the title role of *Orfeo* was created for the castrato Gaetano Guadagni, whose 'ideas of acting were taken. . .from Garrick, who, when he performed in an English opera called the *Fairies,* took. . .pleasure in forming him as an actor' (Burney, *General History,* II, p. 876).

Burney knew Guadagni well. The singer had introduced him to the Dowager Electress of Saxony and, on a tour of her house and gardens, 'Guadagni and Rauzzini [a fellow castrato] sung a great part of the time, particularly in the bath, where there was an excellent room for music' (Burney, *Music in Germany,* p. 50). When we read Burney's account of Guadagni's art, it becomes obvious why Gluck trusted him with the role of Orpheus: 'As an actor, he seems to have had no equal on any stage in Europe. . .his attitudes and gestures were so full of grace and propriety, that they would have been excellent studies for a statuary' (Burney, *General History,* II, p. 876). Burney, moreover, gives us a clue as to where Guadagni employed his 'attitudes and gestures': 'the Music he sung was the most simple imaginable; a few notes with frequent pauses, and opportunities of being liberated from the composer and the band, were all he wanted' (*ibid.*). This suggests quite a different interpretation of the opening chorus of the opera from the immobile tableau we usually see. Perhaps Guadagni interspersed the isolated cries of 'Euridice!' with the expressive mime he learnt from Garrick. Let the Dowager Electress have the last word, in a judgement which would apply as well to Gluck as to his principal singer: 'Guadagni sung with much art, as well as feeling; and had the great secret of hiding defects' (Burney, *Music in Germany,* p. 49).

Garrick's new manner of acting also found favour with one of the most influential theatre reformers of the century, the choreographer Noverre: 'I would like to propose as a model Mr Garrick, the celebrated English actor' (Noverre, *Lettres,* IX). Noverre achieved for the ballet a reform as crucial as Gluck's reform of opera. His search for what was natural and expressive (the same words recur in all the aesthetic discussions of this period, making it difficult to attribute any single concept to its originator) began with his work on Rameau's operas. He abandoned the dance based on abstract movements and geometric patterns in favour of 'dramatic pantomime', closely modelled on Garrick's use of gesture. He required his dancers to forget their steps and to express the soul of the drama ('abandonner leur allure et prendre une âme'). His influential *Lettres sur la danse et sur les ballets* were published in 1760, immediately after his first personal contact with Garrick, and their advocacy of expressive gesture made a profound (though repudiated) impact on the imperial ballet-master Angiolini, the choreographer of *Orfeo.*

Noverre sought also to introduce realism into stage costume. Dress in the eighteenth-century theatre was essentially an extravagant version of current fashion:

The sight was familiar, at Drury Lane, of Banquo's ghost in a powdered wig. . . Lord Mount Edgcumbe, taken when very young to hear Gabrielli as Dido, could remember nothing about her but 'the care with which she tucked up her great hoop as she sidled into the flames of Carthage'. . . Jacopo Ferretti writes: 'I remember to have seen, at the Teatro Argentina, Julius Caesar falling stabbed at the foot of Pompey's statue, shod in elegant ox-tongue shoes with blood red heels and paste buckles, silk stockings with flowers embroidered in colours up the sides, olive-green knee breeches with emerald fastenings, and an incipient rain of ringlets falling about his face.'

(Heriot, *The Castrati in Opera,* pp. 80-1)

Garrick had made the striking innovation of adopting a different costume to play Shylock from the one he wore for Macbeth. The encyclopaedist Diderot strove to have this reform adopted in the French theatre; in *De la poésie dramatique* (Paris, 1758) he wrote: 'What is needed is a few, simple garments in a plain colour, not a vulgar display of brocade.' Noverre freed his dancers from the traditional padded costumes and elaborate head-dresses worn by both the actors at the Comédie-Francaise and the dancers at the Opéra. In their place he designed simple garments which allowed for much more movement, and which also indicated the nationality and social rank of the character. (Voltaire had had to buy the costumes for his play *Orpheline de Chine* out of his own pocket, in order to get something more oriental than the fashions of mid-eighteenth-century Paris!) Some of Noverre's classical costumes scandalised by their skimpy and revealing lines: there was at least some resistance to the ideas of simplicity and realism in pre-Revolutionary Europe.

The innovation of realistic scenery followed closely on the changes in acting and costume. Diderot exhorted: 'Would you have your poets depict the truth in the action and dialogue of your plays, and have your actors return to realistic acting and natural declamation? Then demand that the setting be true to life' (*ibid.*). But before the setting could be allowed to make its full contribution to the drama, the concept of the stage as an intact area representing the scene of the action had to be rediscovered. Theatregoers all over Europe had suffered distraction and blocked views by the presence of spectators on the stage. It was a noted abuse in Molière's day, and one he criticised through his plays:

J'étais sur le théâtre en humeur d'écouter
La pièce, qu'à plusieurs j'avais ouï vanter;
Les acteurs commençaient, chacun prêtait silence,
Lorsque, d'un air bruyant et plein d'extravagance,
Un homme à grands canons est entré brusquement
En criant 'Holà! ho! un siège promptement!'
Et de son grand fracas surprenant l'assemblée,
Dans le plus bel endroit a la pièce troublé...
Mais l'homme pour s'asseoir a fait nouveau fracas,
Et traversant encor le théâtre à grands pas,
Bien que dans les côtés il put être à son aise,
Au milieu du devant il a planté sa chaise,
Et de son large dos morguant les spectateurs,
Aux trois quarts du parterre a caché les acteurs.

I went to the theatre in a mood to hear
The play, which I'd been recommended.
The actors had begun, and the talking ceased,
When, with plenty of noise and bustle,
A man of fashion abruptly entered,
Crying, 'You there — a seat, straight away!'
Disturbing the audience with his uproar

And disrupting the most beautiful part of the play.
In getting to his seat, he made a further commotion,
Striding across the theatre,
And although he could have had a good seat at the side,
He placed his chair right in the front of the stage,
Blocking the view with his bulk,
And obscuring the actors from three-quarters of the pit.

(Molière, *Les fâcheux*, I. 1)

In operatic productions of the early eighteenth century it was the *prima donna*'s mother, maidservant and admirers who crowded the stage, armed with mirrors, combs and smelling salts to restore her between arias. The beginning of the end of this custom adds one more coincidence to the artistic climate which produced *Orfeo:* seats on the stage were abolished at the Comédie-Francaise in 1759 and at the Drury Lane Theatre in 1762.

We have been looking at evidence of a new climate of thought in the theatre, chiefly showing itself in England and in France. But it was in Vienna that the new trends in acting, dance, scenery and costume first came together – in Gluck's masterpiece *Orfeo*. And if we think it in some degree coincidental that Garrick, Diderot, Rousseau, Voltaire and Noverre were all thinking along similar lines in different areas of the continent, how much more impressive is the coincidence which brought Gluck, Calzabigi, Angiolini, Quaglio and Guadagni to Vienna to collaborate in a drama which has proved to be more enduringly successful than any other stage work of the period. Although accounts of how the collaboration came about are contradictory – Calzabigi and Gluck are particularly unreliable in their reminiscences – it is impossible to overlook the part played by Count Durazzo, Intendant of the imperial theatres.

Giacomo Durazzo, who came to Vienna in 1750 as Genoese ambassador, was dedicated to reconciling the traditionally opposed schools of French and Italian music. Since Vienna was a city dominated by Italian culture, this involved importing French works, French artists and French aesthetics. Durazzo never intended to make French culture dominate Vienna as Mazarin had attempted to make Italian culture dominate Paris a century before. He seems to have been genuinely interested in the cross-fertilisation of different artistic traditions. It is typical of his attitude that one of his first acts on coming to Vienna was to adapt Quinault's libretto, *Armide,* written for Lully in Paris some seventy years earlier (and set in its original version by Gluck in 1777), to the Italian taste.

Durazzo engaged Gluck in 1754, to compose and conduct theatre music. It would be interesting to know what qualities he had perceived in Gluck's early music which accounted for the choice. Certainly he used Gluck as a pawn in an artistic war, to break the stranglehold of the composer Hasse and the imperial court poet Metastasio on the Viennese theatre. Such conflicts were common in eighteenth-century Europe: Gluck was to find himself at the centre of an even fiercer one two decades later in Paris.

Burney describes the 'war' in Vienna as it had developed a few years later, when the poet Calzabigi had been added to Durazzo's faction:

Party runs as high among poets, musicians, and their adherents, at Vienna as elsewhere. Metastasio and Hasse, may be said, to be at the head of one of the principal sects; and Calsabigi and Gluck of another. The first, regarding all innovations as quackery, adhere to the ancient form of the musical drama, in which the poet and musician claim equal attention from an audience; the bard in the recitatives and narrative parts; and the composer in the airs, duos and chorusses. The second party depend more on theatrical effects, propriety of character, simplicity of diction, and of musical execution, than on, what *they* style, flowery descriptions, superfluous similes, sententious and cold morality, on one side, with tiresome symphonies, and long divisions, on the other.

(Burney, *Music in Germany*, pp. 81-2)

(By 'tiresome symphonies' and 'long divisions' Burney is criticising arias with long orchestral introductions and over-elaborate vocal ornamentation.) It is as well to remember that before composing *Orfeo*, Gluck had set at least a dozen of Metastasio's texts without, apparently, criticising either their language or their morality. He had also written more than a handful of 'tiresome symphonies' and 'long divisions' himself.

It is perhaps for this reason that Durazzo surrounded Gluck with creative artists in touch with the new trends in theatrical thought. But first he made his own contribution to Gluck's personal enlightenment. In 1755 they collaborated in writing a one-act opera, *L'innocenza giustificata*. Durazzo compiled a libretto by bringing together some rather bland aria texts by Metastasio (drawn from several different operas) and writing the recitatives himself. In this work, he was able to show Gluck the superiority of action over lyricism when he made two of the characters rush on stage to interrupt a grandiose prayer aria with news of the victim's deliverance.

It seems as if Durazzo next decided to teach Gluck the virtues of simplicity. The importation of French comic operas to the imperial court started a craze. Gluck began by conducting little comedies, with words by the French dramatist Favart and with French traditional and popular airs. He was soon composing his own settings, and while the best of these are quite elaborate small-scale operas, the vocal style remains syllabic, the forms miniaturised, and the characters realistically contemporary — peasant lovers, shrewish wives, credulous drunkards — in contrast to the 'cold' and 'sententious' historical figures of Metastasian *opera seria.*

The choreographer Gasparo Angiolini arrived in Vienna before Gluck, to work under the imperial ballet-master, Hilverding, whose ideas of dramatic mime and expressive dance Angiolini later accused Noverre of plagiarising. And when in 1761 Durazzo introduced Gluck to the scene-painter Giovanni Maria Quaglio, the castrato singer Gaetano Guadagni and the poet Ranieri de' Calzabigi, the cast was assembled. Representatives of all the new dramatic theories which were permeating Europe had come together, partly by design, partly by sheer coincidence, to set the stage for the musically and historically significant reform of opera.

Calzabigi and Metastasio

A great opportunist, well versed in financial operations, familiar with the commerce of all nations, learned in history, wit, poet and great lover of women.

(Casanova of Calzabigi, *Mémoires*, II, p. 30)

Calzabigi was one of many colourful, libertine adventurers in the artistic world of the eighteenth century, leading, in common with Mozart's librettist Lorenzo da Ponte, and with Casanova himself, a life sufficiently eventful for a picaresque novel, and yet making a genuine and lasting contribution to art. Born in Leghorn in 1714, he was exactly of an age with Gluck, and was exposed to much the same influences. When, in Milan in the 1740s, Gluck was selecting for his first operas texts by the most famous librettist of the day, the imperial court poet Pietro Metastasio, Calzabigi, in Naples, was producing libretti modelled closely on Metastasio's poems. At least one of these early libretti he sent to the imperial court poet, who thereafter encouraged him and even collaborated with him in a collected edition of his (Metastasio's) dramatic poems, published in Paris in 1755 with sycophantic preface by Calzabigi.

Calzabigi had fled to Paris in 1750, following trial for murder in Naples. He nevertheless arrived in the French capital in the role of secretary to the ambassador of Naples. Police records describe him as 'tall, thin and brown, aged about thirty years, well ordered and extremely withdrawn' (Paris, Bibliothèque de l'Arsénal MS 10293). Casanova explains his reticence: 'I found him unappetising, afflicted with a kind of leprosy, though that did not prevent him either from eating or from writing. . .he was a good conversationalist and an entertaining fellow' *(Mémoires,* II, p. 29). While in Paris, Calzabigi continued in his career as poet. In 1752 he published the libretto of a cantata by Bambini in which he is described as 'known in Madrid for the success of his dramatic poems'. It was probably this work which brought him to the notice of Madame de Pompadour, whose protection played an important part in his subsequent activities. In 1755 the collected edition of Metastasio's poems was launched, dedicated to la Pompadour, and containing the celebrated preface in which Calzabigi on the one hand lauded the perfection of Metastasio's dramatic scheme while at the same time pointing out the superiority of the French operatic tradition:

Whenever [the ground-plan of French opera] is reconciled with truth, whenever purely human actions are unfolded to the exclusion of pagan divinities, devilry and magic – in a word, all that is beyond human control – there is no doubt that with a large chorus, a corps de ballet and scenery which is strongly allied to both the poetry and the music, a splendid result could be obtained in which the spectator would be moved simultaneously by the variety and magnificence of the visual display, the interest of the plot, the delicacy of the poetry and the seductive sweetness of the music.

Calzabigi's career was built, however, on the two interests of poetry and commerce. Finding that publication was unlikely to make his fortune, he became drawn into Madame de Pompadour's business concerns, and at her request organised a lottery in partnership with his brother and Casanova, to defray the expenses of the new École Militaire at Vincennes. Such schemes were common in eighteenth-century Europe – Calzabigi's brother was later to mount a similar venture on behalf of Frederick the Great – and were almost invariably corrupt. It is highly probable that when Calzabigi left Paris in 1760 he was under threat of expulsion for fraud. But when he arrived within twelve months in Vienna, the 'great opportunist' had again acquired a position of respectability as privy councillor to the Netherlands at the Treasury in Vienna, where his immediate superior, Prince Kaunitz, introduced him to the musical and theatrical life of the imperial city.

To understand Calzabigi's significance in the history of opera, we need to know something of Metastasio, the poet he began by imitating and later denounced. Most writings about Gluck emphasise the 'establishment' status of Metastasio's work and the 'revolutionary' nature of Calzabigi's reforms to such an extent that it is easy to overlook the fact that Metastasio had been in his time a reformer of opera.

Opera has always been highly susceptible to fashion. It is a constantly developing genre, its emphasis changing, in roughly fifty-year cycles, between the poet and the musician. In the late seventeenth century it had given temporary supremacy to the designer and machinist, and it is this mode of opera that Metastasio, with his older contemporary Zeno, changed:

As the British government consists of three estates: King, Lords, and Commons, so an opera in its first institution consisted of Poetry, Music, and Machinery: but as politicians have observed, that the ballance of power is frequently disturbed by some one of the three estates encroaching upon the other two, so one of these three constituent parts of a musical drama generally preponderates, at the expence of the other two. In the first operas POETRY seems to have been the most important personage; but about the middle of the last century, MACHINERY and DECORATION seemed to take the lead, and diminished the importance both of Music and poetry. But as the art of singing and dramatic composition improved, MUSIC took the lead, and poetry and decoration became of less consequence, till the judgment of Apostolo Zeno, and the genius of Metastasio, lifted lyric poetry far above its usual level.

(Burney, *General History*, II, p. 892)

The structure of Metastasian opera owed much to the dramatic tradition of Racine and, more particularly, Corneille. All the hallmarks of French classical drama are there: a small cast of neatly paired lovers and confidants, the conflict of love and duty, and improbable instances of clemency and self-sacrifice bringing about the resolution. Metastasio's dramas depended on the detailed portrayal of character through a series of set pieces — a string of highly conventional aria types whose distribution and sequence soon became a convention in itself. The arias became the drama. The externals of elaborate machinery and machines were abandoned.

Metastasio also 'purified' opera by removing the comic characters (and incidentally giving impetus to the new, separate genre of comic opera): 'the mixture of comic scenes in serious musical dramas prevailed in most of the early operas, and even oratorios. . .and continued to disgrace them till banished by the better taste and sounder judgment of Apostolo Zeno and Metastasio, who convinced the public that such buffoonery was unnecessary' (*ibid.* p. 546).

Metastasio's letters suggest, however, that he was more concerned with diplomacy than with musico-dramatic theory. He often has to advise theatre managers on how to deal with the temperamental singers and their constant jealousies. In letters to Pasquini, the manager of the theatre at Dresden, he has to adjudicate which positions the singers should take on stage:

> *'Demofoonte', Act I*
>
> Scene 1
> Matusio   Dircea
>
> Scene 2
> Dircea   Timante
>
> Scene 3
> Adrasto   Demofoonte   Timante

and goes on to explain:

At times, when necessary, the more notable character may be on the left, but this should not produce any inconvenience. In the first place the right side is not universally considered to be the most honoured position; and even if it were, the character could make the left side the more distinguished simply by crossing the stage.

In his next letter the problem still seems to be giving trouble:

If the more notable character is on the left and the lesser one on the right they can still be variously distinguished by placing the former a few paces downstage of the latter.

> (Metastasio, *Lettere,* 16 February 1748)

Metastasio, then, is associated with an operatic convention. His was a comparatively simple form of opera – simple, that is, as to staging, characters and musical structure, for the plots were often absurdly complex, requiring two if not three sets of lovers to suffer misunderstandings and conflicts before the usual happy ending. All that concerns us here is the musical structure: an alternation of recitative and aria only briefly varied by a perfunctory chorus to bring about a festal conclusion. Whatever the plot, the drama was always constructed in a similar way, with a chain of short scenes, each one opening with a passage in prose to explain the action, to be set as recitative, and culminating in the metrical text of an aria, after which the character who had sung it left the stage. The number and distribution of arias was part of the convention, and the librettist's skill consisted as much in arranging the plot so that the proportions (of three arias for the 'first man', two for the 'second man', one for the 'third man') were retained, as in producing elegant verse for the texts of the arias.

Exactly when and how Calzabigi came to disagree with Metastasio's operatic formula is not documented. It seems clear, though, that when he went to Paris in 1750 he was a devoted admirer of the imperial court poet's dramatic art, and saw his path to success as lying in the cultivation of Metastasio's goodwill; when he left Paris ten years later, exposure to the operas of Lully and Rameau had made an indelible impression which was to influence his concept of opera for the remainder of his life.

Certainly *Orfeo* was written out of Calzabigi's convictions that 'with a large chorus, a corps de ballet and scenery which is strongly allied to both the poetry and the music, a splendid result could be obtained'. Planned, and possibly written, while Calzabigi was still in Paris, the poem shows the unmistakable influence of French opera. True, the 'exclusion of pagan divinities' proved too radical for Calzabigi, but at least it is the unfolding of 'purely human actions' on which the plot depends. The novelty of the libretto is apparent from a glance at the plot. Compared with *all* previous operatic versions of the Orpheus legend, it shows a great simplification. The extent to which Calzabigi eliminated unnecessary incidents from the action is strikingly shown by the point at which he opens the drama: not at Orpheus's wedding, not at Eurydice's death, but with the burial already having taken place, so attention is immediately focused on Orpheus himself. Calzabigi's *Orfeo* is a psychological drama: the crucial action takes place within the protagonist's mind. However prominent the intervention of Cupid, however concrete the manifestation of the underworld, however assertive the reactions of Eurydice, it was surely Calzabigi's intention to explore intense emotional states, and to make Orpheus's capacity for sorrow and joy the heart of the drama – an intention which Gluck's very fine choral writing sometimes obscures.

Everything works to focus the drama on a single protagonist. Compared with the six-soloist convention of *opera seria,* Calzabigi's cast-list is revolutionary. There are nominally three soloists, but the roles of Cupid and Eurydice are so slight that they in no way detract from the calculated predominance of Orpheus. Each scene is built around the simple apposition of Orpheus with one other character:

Orpheus and the mourning chorus
Orpheus and Cupid
Orpheus and the Furies
Orpheus and the Blessed Spirits
Orpheus and Eurydice
Orpheus and Cupid
Orpheus and an ensemble consisting of Eurydice, Cupid and the
rejoicing chorus.

Calzabigi uses this series of encounters either to reinforce or to highlight by contrast Orpheus's state of mind.

Deliberately rejecting the improbable and manufactured complexities of Metastasian opera, Calzabigi depicts only recognisable, universal situations. Consequently there are no individualised characters. If we met Calzabigi's Orpheus in the street we would not recognise him – in the sense that we might recognise Poppaea, Susanna or Peter Grimes. To this extent there is no 'characterisation' in *Orfeo*. But in another sense, everyone we meet is a potential Orpheus. The revelation of humanity and common experience in Calzabigi's poem is a strong factor in the opera's greatness, though we in the twentieth century may find it paradoxical that Calzabigi chose to reveal these human truths through the person of a demi-god in his contacts with and largely in worlds other than our own.

Calzabigi and Gluck

It is not easy to establish what happened between Gluck and Calzabigi in the year 1762. Neither was reluctant to talk about the collaboration. But most of the sources date from some years after *Orfeo* had become an acknowledged success, when both creative artists had an interest in claiming credit for the invention of the new style of opera. Moreover, we cannot be completely sure of the authorship of every source: it is widely accepted that Calzabigi probably wrote the preface to *Alceste* which appears over Gluck's name, and which attributes much of the success of his operas to the qualities of the libretti. On the other hand, Gluck is even more generous to Calzabigi in a letter to the *Mercure de France*, written long after their collaboration had finished, and when he was under no apparent pressure to give a misleading account. Perhaps the truth of the matter is that any artistic collaboration is a complex affair, and neither man quite knew where his influence began and ended.

It seems reasonable, then, to let the sources tell their own story. The following pages bring together, I believe for the first time, all the principal occasions on which either Gluck or Calzabigi described the genesis of *Orfeo*. (Where no source is given the letters are translated from transcripts lent me by the late Egon Wellesz.)

Calzabigi to Prince Kaunitz, Vienna, 6 March 1767

Matters are entirely different in the new plan of musical drama which has been, if not invented, at least put into practice by me in *Orfeo*, then in *Alceste*, and continued by Signor Coltellini. All is nature here, all is passion; there are no sententious reflections, no philosophy or politics, no paragons of virtue, and none of those descriptions or amplifications which are only an avoidance of difficulties and are to be found in all libretti. The duration is limited to what does not tire or make the attention wander. The [plot is] simple, not romanticised; a few verses are enough to inform the spectators of the progress of the action which is never complicated or duplicated in servile, uncalled-for obedience to the silly rule concerning the *secundo uomo* and the *seconda donna,* but reduced to the dimensions of Greek tragedy, and therefore has the unique advantage of exciting terror and compassion in the same way as spoken tragedy. According to this plan, as your Highness will perceive, the music has no other function than to express what arises from the words, which are therefore neither smothered by notes nor used to lengthen the spectacle unduly, because it is ridiculous to prolong the sentence 'I love you' (for instance) with a hundred notes when nature has restricted it to three. (I am of the opinion that a note can never have the value of more than one syllable.)

(Quoted in Hammelmann and Rose, 'New Light on Calzabigi')

This letter, the earliest source on the working relationship of Gluck and Calzabigi that we have, is a plea, from a practical man of the theatre to the management, to perform Gluck's operas with suitable singers or not at all — *'Orfeo* went well, because there we had Guadagni' (*ibid.*) Clearly, it was written before Calzabigi acquired an inflated opinion of his role in the reform: towards the end of the letter he actually describes his next opera, *Alceste,* as 'this child of my poor genius and Signor Gluck's sublime gifts'. He was never to assess their respective merits in such language again.

The *Alceste* preface, referred to above, deals, of course, principally with the second fruit of the collaboration. However, it is such an important source for the changes Gluck and Calzabigi introduced into opera, and refers to the working relationship in such unbiased, if unspecific, language, that it forms an essential part of our compilation.

Calzabigi/Gluck to the Grand Duke of Tuscany, Vienna, 1769

I resolved to free music from all the abuses that have crept in either through mistaken vanity on the part of singers, or through excessive complaisance on the part of composers. . .I sought to restrict the music to its true purpose of expressing the poetry and supporting the action, without interrupting the story or holding it up with unnecessary and superfluous ornamentation. . .I have tried to avoid stopping an actor in the heat of a dialogue in order to interrupt him with a tedious ritornello, or to hold him up in the middle of a word merely so that he might show off the flexibility of his voice in a long roulade, or to make him wait while the orchestra gives him time to collect his breath for a cadenza. . .These are my principles. By good fortune, all my intentions were aided admirably by the libretto, in which the celebrated author, having devised a new scheme for the drama, had replaced florid descriptions, artificial similes, sententious and frigid morality with the language of the heart, with strong passions, lively situations, and ever-varied spectacle.

(Preface to *Alceste*)

A distinct change of tone is discernible in the next source. In a letter to the editor of the *Mercure de France*, Gluck sought to recommend himself and his work to the directors of the Paris opera house (the Académie Royale de Musique). Here, for the first time, the 'principal merit' is attributed to Calzabigi.

Gluck to the *Mercure de France*, Vienna, 1 February 1773

I would lay myself open to just reproach if. . .I agreed to accept the credit for having invented the new form of Italian opera, which has proved so successful an experiment. It is to M. de Calzabigi that the principal merit belongs, and if my music has met with some approval, I feel bound to confess that it is to him I am indebted, for it is he who made it possible for me to explore the resources of my art. This author, full of genius and talent, has in his poems *Orphée*, *Alceste* and *Paris* devised a form which is quite unknown to the Italians. These works are composed of striking situations, exploiting those elements of terror and pathos which provide the composer with the opportunity to express great passion and to write strong and stirring music. However talented the composer, he will never create more than mediocre music if the poet fails to arouse in him that enthusiasm without which all art is weak and lifeless.

If we want to discover why Gluck was behaving with such apparent disinterest in this account, we have only to read the rest of the letter, in which he associates himself at a stroke with both 'the famous M. Rousseau of Geneva' and the still highly regarded seventeenth-century composer Lully. It seems that Gluck, endeavouring to ingratiate himself with the Parisian public, had decided to show his knowledge of and connections with all that they esteemed. And he must have thought that by giving credit to Calzabigi, who had first made a name for himself in Paris, he was supplying yet another reason for the Parisians to welcome him.

Gluck's statement in this letter made it impossible for him to refute Calzabigi's more extreme claims in subsequent years. The fullest account the poet ever gave of their working relationship appears in another letter to the *Mercure de France:*

Calzabigi to the *Mercure de France*, Naples, 25 June 1784

I arrived in Vienna in 1761, full of these ideas [for a new kind of opera based on declamation]. A year later, Count Durazzo, the then director of entertainments at the imperial court and today its ambassador at Venice, to whom I had recited my poem *Orpheus*, persuaded me to have it performed in the theatre. I agreed on the condition that the music should be written according to my ideas. He sent me M. Gluck who, he said, would suit my taste. At that time, M. Gluck was not held to be one of our finest composers — no doubt this was an erroneous judgement. Hasse, Buranello, Jommelli, Peres and others were at the top of the tree. None of them understood what I meant by 'declamatory music'; and as for M. Gluck, who did not pronounce our language very well, it would have been impossible for him to declaim even a few lines as they should be spoken. I read him my poem *Orpheus*, and by reading and rereading several passages to him, I was able to show him the nuances I put into my expression, the pauses, the slowness, the quickness, the intonation, now stressed, now level and glossed over, which I desired him to incorporate in his setting. At the same time, I begged him to banish passage-work, cadenzas, ritornelli and all the gothic and barbaric extravagances that have crept into our music. M. Gluck went along with my ideas. . .I hope that you will concede, Monsieur, after this explanation, that if M. Gluck is the creator of Dramatic Opera, he has not created it out of nothing. I furnished him with the basic ingredients — the chaos, if you will. The honours of creation are thus equally shared between us.

Two important claims are made here: that Calzabigi had written and semi-publicly recited his poem before he ever met Gluck, and that he had to teach Gluck how to set the Italian text. There seems to be no evidence for or against the first claim. The second gives rise to some interesting considerations. Certainly in the collected edition of Calzabigi's works published in 1774 the 'signs' clarifying the declamation can be seen, and Gluck's recitative follows these indications to the letter. Moreover, in his letter of 1773 quoted above, Gluck disclaimed an intimate knowledge of the Italian language: 'born in Germany, I believe that whatever study I have made of the Italian language, as also of the French, is insufficient to enable me to appreciate the delicate nuances which make the one preferable to the other'. It is surely absurd, however, to suggest that Gluck should have needed Calzabigi's coaching when by 1762 he had set at least twenty-three Italian texts, and given rise to no surviving criticism of his handling of the language — a language which in eighteenth century Europe was as universally known as English is today.

Some insight into the way Gluck handled a text can be deduced from his better-documented collaborations with other librettists. In advising his friend Christoph Wieland on how to construct an opera libretto based on Shakespeare's *Antony and Cleopatra*, Gluck is shrewdly practical:

Gluck to Wieland, Vienna, 7 August 1776

All I ask is that instead of the usual confidants, you should introduce choruses, of Romans on Antony's side and Egyptian women on Cleopatra's. Confidants or other secondary characters make the play dull. A further reason is that it is rarely easy to find more than one good soprano singer. Choruses, however, are lively and make a splendid effect when they fill the stage, particularly at the end.

When he discusses the ending of the French version of *Alceste* with his librettist du Roullet (*Alceste*, like *Orfeo*, exists in two distinct versions, one for Vienna, one for Paris), Gluck seems to be thinking of his characters as real people. He is less concerned with effect than with emotion and nature:

Gluck to du Roullet, Vienna, 2 December 1775

Your chorus are always active and the piece revolves very much around them in the first two acts, for they are unwilling to lose such a perfect king and queen. But in the third act the chorus, who took so much interest in preserving their sovereigns, do not appear, and are quite forgotten. I say that the opera cannot end until these poor people have been consoled. It is no good telling me that Apollo brings them back. This seems to me to be an *hors d'œuvre* brought about very artificially. . . In my ending everything is brought about naturally, without any need for miracles.

Gluck's growing confidence in dealing with librettists is evident in his relationship with Guillard, the author of *Iphigénie en Tauride:*

Gluck to Guillard, Vienna, 17 June 1778

I want lines of ten syllables, and take care to put a long and sonorous syllable wherever I indicate.

These sources show something of the size of the librettist's and the composer's joint task. From the engagement of suitable singers to the number of syllables necessary to get the chorus from one side of the stage to the other, opera is a collaboration. Of no single achievement of the reform can we say, 'Gluck did this'. There is always an equal possibility that the credit is due elsewhere.

3 *Synopsis*

BY PATRICIA HOWARD

It is obviously outside the scope of this volume to investigate the literary merits of the libretto – and in any case such an investigation might well be inappropriate, since, notwithstanding his account of reciting the work to Durazzo before Gluck came on the scene, Calzabigi designed his poem to be set and sung, not read. Its importance is as a ground-plan for an opera.

It also provides some evidence that the novelty of *Orfeo,* and its reform characteristics, were stimulated by the librettist. We shall find several moments in the opera where Calzabigi's dramatic touch is surer than Gluck's: and nowhere is this more apparent than in the overture. Later in his career, Gluck was to make the operatic overture an eloquent introduction to the following drama, establishing the mood of the opening scene and even attempting to 'set forth its argument' (preface to *Alceste*) – though Berlioz later pointed out the impossibility of the latter claim. *Orfeo,* however, was written before Gluck conceived this wholly revolutionary idea. Its overture is a jolly, bustling affair in C major, indistinguishable from the overtures to his earlier operas, and totally unrelated to the mood of the drama. It has remained an enduring embarrassment. Several subsequent productions have attempted to remedy it: at a performance by the students of the Milan Conservatoire on 19 May 1813, the powerfully tragic overture to *Iphigénie en Aulide* was substituted, and as recently as 16 January 1961, Colin Graham's production at Covent Garden, conducted by Louis de Froment, abandoned the overture altogether. Calzabigi, though, had arranged for a more appropriate introduction. His directions read, 'The curtain rises to the sound of a melancholy symphony. . .'

The stage represents a 'pleasant but lonely grove of laurels and cypresses' where nymphs and shepherds are carrying out funeral rites at the tomb of Eurydice. After the orchestral introduction – the 'melan-choly symphony' – the chorus sings a mourning hymn, interrupted by three anguished cries of 'Euridice!' from the bereaved Orpheus. The

27

scene cannot fail to make the most intense impression. The tone colour of the opening symphony is curiously solemn, with its scoring for cornetti (already archaic in 1762) and alto, tenor and bass trombones besides the basic strings and continuo. When the chorus sings the same material, the effect is subdued, owing to the comparatively low pitch of the soprano line and the close compass of the vocal parts. Only the three cries of Orpheus are thrown into relief against this dark background. We know that when he was rehearsing the Paris production of 1774, Gluck instructed the singer Le Gros to scream these cries, 'as if someone is sawing through your bone!' (quoted in Mannlich, *Ein deutscher Maler,* p. 274).

In a short recitative passage, Orpheus urges his companions to finish their ceremonies, and a marvellously tender, caressing ballet movement is danced before the return of the opening chorus, sung this time without Orpheus's cries, and constructed to make a palindrome with the first statement, in that the 'melancholy symphony' follows rather than precedes the chorus, giving the mourners time to retire.

This scene is one of several in the opera that shows the influence of Calzabigi's years in Paris, and his familiarity with French *tragédie lyrique*. Nothing on this time-scale was being written in Italian opera. It is not just that Calzabigi has replaced the mechanical Metastasian alternation of recitative and aria with a greatly enlarged role for the chorus: there is integration of every element into a visual and aural unity. The music is a continuous whole, bound together not only by the musical and dramatic involvement of Orpheus with the chorus, but by the repetition of the chorus to impose an overall form on the scene, by the string accompaniment which continues throughout the recitative, and by the ternary key scheme of

C minor (symphony, chorus and recitative)
E flat major (ballet)
C minor (chorus and symphony)

Left alone, Orpheus adds his individual voice to the formal rites that have taken place. 'Chiamo il mio ben così', he sings ('I call thus upon my love'). Only an echo answers him. We are reminded of this fruitless calling for Eurydice later, in the last act, when she calls, equally unheeded, for Orpheus to turn to her. There are two great laments in *Orfeo:* this three-strophe song, and the celebrated 'Che farò senza Euridice?' ('What shall I do without Eurydice?'). Both are restrained utterances compared with the recitative passages that intersperse the verses of 'Chiamo' and precede 'Che farò', and compared with the three cries of 'Euridice!' in the first chorus. Throughout the opera we need to remember that the hero is not only a husband but the god of song. (The castrato voice of the original Orpheus would have underlined this point.) There is a distancing formality in his solo arias, and a simplicity of line that can make them seem too detached for drama. Moreover, both numbers are in a major key, which we might be tempted to think insufficiently expressive of tragedy – until we remember that Gluck's contemporaries had no such limited concepts. Gluck's great idol, Handel, set his moments of greatest pathos in major keys ('He was despisèd' in *Messiah*, 'Waft her, angels' in *Jephtha*), and Orpheus's mourning here is no less intense. When Orpheus exclaims,

> Ma sola al mio dolor
> l'eco risponde

> But alone to my grief
> Echo replies

we hear the echo in an off-stage orchestra (featuring more archaic instruments, the reedy chalumeaux): an effect very dear to seventeenth- and eighteenth-century composers, but none the less poignant.

After the close of the third verse of the song, Orpheus's grief turns to anger against the 'barbari numi. . .avida delle morti' ('barbarous gods. . .greedy for deaths'). In an agitated recitative, he resolves to defy the tyrant gods and, following in the footsteps of the great heroes, descend to the horrors of the underworld to reclaim his wife. It is a stirring passage; Orpheus's resolution is supported by fierce string accompaniment (in the tradition of the *stile concitato* of early baroque opera). At the end of the recitative there seems no clear reason why Orpheus should not set off at once for the underworld, abduct Eurydice and return with her to live happily ever after. But myths are rarely so straightforward. There has to be a twist in the chain of events, an additional condition to be complied with. The arrival of Cupid can seem redundant to a twentieth-century audience. The libretto does not make it clear whether he descends in a machine or enters disguised as a shepherd (which has become traditional for his parallel intervention in the last act), but in either case he intrudes upon the grief of the bereaved husband, destroying the verisimilitude the drama has established up to this point. We have to be careful not to react anachronistically here. When Calzabigi replaced Metastasio's quasi-realistic historical plots with myths, he claimed that he was turning not away from but towards 'truth' and 'nature'. For an eighteenth-century writer, as much as for his audience, the important consideration was the emotional range of Orpheus's role, and the device of Cupid's intervention was acceptable because it provided Orpheus with a wholly new torment in the third act.

Cupid, then, announces that Jove has taken pity on Orpheus's plight, and permits him to descend, living, into the realm of the dead, where, if Orpheus can placate the Furies with his singing, Eurydice will be restored to him. As soon as Orpheus has expressed his rapture at this concession, however, Cupid announces a further test:

> Euridice ti si vieta il mirar
> Finchè non sei fuor degli antri di Stige!
> E il gran divieto rivelarle non dei
> Se no, la perdi, e di nuovo, e per sempre.

> You are forbidden to look at Eurydice
> Until you are beyond the caves of the Styx!
> And you must not reveal this great prohibition
> Or else you will lose her, once more and for ever.

Something superhuman is being asked of Orpheus here, and if we are aware of the magnitude of the test, we shall find the third act the more agonising. The degree of heroism needed for the living to enter the underworld has been memorably depicted in many operas, and perhaps nowhere more movingly than in Gluck's own opera *Alceste,* where the heroine voluntarily braves the horrors of death, not to rescue, but to become a substitute for, her dying husband. But more than this physical bravery is asked of Orpheus. In having to turn away from Eurydice at the moment when he finds her, and in the sadistic rider that he must not explain this behaviour, Orpheus is being asked to display an *un-natural* degree of self-control. And since the first scene has demonstrated the strength of his *natural* feelings, we realise that he is bound to fail this test.

The little aria which Cupid sings before leaving Orpheus is disarming in music and text. He attempts to deny the inevitability of the tragedy, arguing that 'Sometimes in the presence of the loved one, lovers are struck blind and dumb in their trembling confusion.'

> Sai purche talora
> confusi, tremanti,
> con chi gl'innamora
> son ciechi gli amanti
> non sanno parlar.

In other words, the behaviour imposed on Orpheus is, after all, only natural! (An exploration of what is 'nature' and what constitutes 'natural' emotions and behaviour forms a recurrent theme not only in *Orfeo* but in many operas and literary works of the century, from *The*

Beggar's Opera to *Così fan tutte,* and from Pope to Wordsworth.)

Alone once more, Orpheus restores the tension by imagining not the conventional behaviour of lovers meeting, suggested by Cupid, but his actual and specific reunion with Eurydice: 'Preveggo...comprendo...' – he foresees her anguish, and vividly envisages his own distress. (In Act III, when Eurydice first upbraids him, Orpheus exclaims, 'Lo preveddi' ('I foresaw it'). The anticipation of disaster doubles its pain.) Realising, however, that it would be an even greater torment to live deprived of 'the unique object of his soul's affection' ('privo dell'unico dell'alma amato oggetto'), he accepts the gods' condition, and disappears in a clap of thunder. A rushing passage for strings depicts his descent into Hades.

The second act opens in a 'horrid cavern' beyond the Styx. The air is thick with smoke and fire. Calzabigi called for an 'orribile sinfonia' and Gluck responded with a prelude embodying both nobility and terror. The dance of the Infernal Spirits is broken off as they hear the approach of Orpheus:

> Chi mai dell'Erebo
> fra le caligini
> sull'orme d'Ercole
> e di Piritoo
> conduce il piè?
>
> D'orror l'ingombrino,
> le fiere Eumenidi,
> e lo spaventino
> gli urli di Cerbero
> se un dio non è.

> Whoever through
> the darkness of Erebus
> in the footsteps of Hercules
> and Pirithous
> wanders?
>
> Fill him with horror,
> fierce Furies,
> Frighten him with
> the howls of Cerberus
> if he be not a god.

This chorus is sung before and after a threatening dance movement. Then the opening 'symphony of terror' returns, to be interrupted as before with the harp and plucked strings representing the sound of Orpheus's lyre.

Orfeo is full of significant parallels, some of them constructed by

Gluck, but most of them built into the libretto by Calzabigi. Into the calm and confident beauty of Orpheus's first aria, the Furies interject angry cries, which remind us of Orpheus's own interpolations in the opening chorus of the opera:

Orpheus:	Deh! placatevi con me,
	Furie,
Chorus:	Nò!
Orpheus:	Larve,
Chorus:	Nò!
Orpheus:	Ombre sdegnose;
Chorus:	Nò!
Orpheus:	Vi renda almen pietose
	il mio barbaro dolor,
Chorus:	Nò! Nò! Nò!

Orpheus:	Ah! be appeased,
	Furies,
Chorus:	No!
Orpheus:	Spirits,
Chorus:	No!
Orpheus:	Scornful Shades;
Chorus:	No!
Orpheus:	At least take pity on
	my cruel anguish,
Chorus:	No! No! No!

In spite of their fierce denials, the Furies are susceptible to Orpheus's singing. Abandoning their attempts to frighten him, they warn him of the weeping and groaning that fill the underworld. Orpheus replies that he already shares their suffering: 'Ho con me l'inferno mio' ('I have my own hell within me'). The Furies are moved by his gentleness, and in a hushed chorus they express their pity for him. As their music becomes calm, Orpheus's pleading becomes more agitated:

> Men tiranne ah! voi sareste
> al mio pianto, al mio dolor,
> se provaste un sol momento
> cosa sia languir d'amor.

> Ah, you would be less cruel
> to my tears and my grief
> if you had felt for one single moment
> what it is to die of love.

With this plea, Orpheus overcomes. The hushed chorus is repeated, rising to a climax as the gates are flung open, and fading away again into a distant murmur as the Furies withdraw. Calzabigi is quite specific on this point: 'The Furies and monsters begin to retire, dispersing within, repeating the final verse of the chorus, which continues while they fade away, ending finally in a confused murmur.' Nothing could be clearer than this verbal instruction, and Gluck's ending of the chorus follows it exactly, the dynamic dropping from piano to pianissimo and the four-part singing contracting to two parts and then to a single line for the last bars. Composer and librettist, it would seem, were working hand in hand.

Why, then, in the revision of *Orfeo* for Paris in 1774, did Gluck destroy this eloquent portrayal of the pacified Furies by bringing them back in their full vigour to dance an extra ballet movement before the fall of the curtain? Pressure to conform to local taste must have been very strong to force the composer to obliterate such a carefully constructed dramatic effect. Or was it that, after all, Gluck felt less passionately about his drama than his biographers are tempted to claim?

The second act of *Orfeo* is the most simply and the most beautifully constructed of all opera acts. After the underworld, the Elysian fields; after darkness and terror, light and bliss. It is a curious fact about music – at least, western European music of the tonal era – that it seems easier to express in it fear, misery and pain than their converse. Music which is merely happy is common enough, but the expression of a supernatural blessedness is rare. One of the great strengths of *Orfeo*, and surely one of the reasons which keep it in the repertoire despite the manifold difficulties of performing it, is the second scene of Act II.

Gluck had many musical limitations, among others, his naive and simplistic orchestration; but the ballet that opens the scene is a miracle of Elysian tone colour. The two flutes and upper strings weave a random sharing of tune and accompaniment to produce an unearthly dance, far removed from its courtly minuet origins. This dance depicts the paradisal landscape, and the following number, Orpheus's bemused and ecstatic reaction to it:

> Che puro ciel,
> Che chiaro sol,
> Che nuova serena luce
> è questa mai!

> How pure the sky,
> How bright the sun,
> What new, serene light
> is this?

Orpheus's words are almost buried in one of the most complex orchestral textures Gluck ever constructed. Too complex, perhaps, to be performed safely, for Gluck simplified the scoring when he revised the opera for Parma in 1769, and this simplification was retained in the Paris score of 1774. It is surprising to discover that such a mature movement has its origins in an aria from one of Gluck's early operas. The basic material of 'Che puro ciel' — that is, the tune and the rippling accompaniment — appears in *Ezio* (1750) and was used again in *Antigone* (1756). But the differences between these earlier versions and the *Orfeo* aria are revealing: in both *Ezio* and *Antigone,* the prominent melody is given to the singer; in *Orfeo* it is played by the oboe, and the voice merely interjects phrases of recitative — an orchestral tone poem with vocal commentary, expressing a personal reaction to the depicted mood (see below, p. 47). Here is another parallel with the first choruses in Act I and Act II: the idea of a dialogue — between Orpheus and the mourners, Orpheus and the Furies, and here, Orpheus and Elysium itself — links the structural building-blocks of the first two acts of the opera.

Gluck sustains this other-worldly mood through a tender chorus of Blessed Spirits:

> Vieni a' regni del riposo,
> grande eroe, tenero sposo.

> Come to the kingdom of repose,
> Great hero, loving spouse.

In order to delay the conflict between them, Calzabigi postponed the meeting between Orpheus and Eurydice to the very end of the act. So the chorus, which claims, 'Cupid gives you back your Eurydice', is followed by a further ballet movement, and Orpheus, not unreasonably, becomes restless:

> Anime avventurose,
> ah tollerate in pace
> le impazienze mie!
> Se foste amanti,
> conoscerete a prova
> quel focoso desio
> che mi tormenta
> che per tutto è con me.

> Fortunate spirits,
> ah, bear patiently
> my impatience!
> If you were lovers,
> you would know yourselves
> what burning desire
> torments me
> and overmasters me.

'During a reprise of their chorus, the Blessed Spirits restore Eurydice to Orpheus:

> Non lagnarti di tua sorte,
> che può dirsi un altro eliso
> uno sposo si fedel.

('Do not regret your fate, so faithful a husband may be called a second Elysium.') This is a significant comparison for Calzabigi's telling of the Orpheus story, and anticipates the happy ending, which has been called an anticlimax, but which is carefully prepared for throughout the libretto. The ending of Calzabigi's drama is very different from all previous versions of the myth. Orpheus's reward, in this opera, is not apotheosis but a restored, human bride, and a new earthly marriage. In choosing this happy ending, Calzabigi was surely intending to replace the baroque solution of Striggio's libretto with a modern, rational, enlightened ending. The opera sets out to show that what is important about Orpheus is his role as a husband, and the plot cannot end without satisfying him on a natural and human level.

After receiving Eurydice's hand, Orpheus leads her away without looking at her. Eurydice, in Calzabigi's scheme, does not sing in the second act. (In the Paris score, she has an aria at the opening of scene 2.) This keeps the attention focused on Orpheus and avoids anticipating Eurydice's characterisation. Eurydice exists only in relation to Orpheus. (Indeed, she is literally dead until he brings her out of the underworld.) When Gluck gave her a sweet, Elysian aria in his Paris score, he made her fierce upbraiding of Orpheus in the last act less credible.

In Act III, Calzabigi's scheme of grand tableaux, with scenes involving chorus, dance and soloist, is abandoned. The essential action takes place between Orpheus and Eurydice alone. A chorus is unthinkable, and dance irrelevant. Through the whim of the gods, Orpheus must undergo a terrible trial which — because of the very tenderness and passion he has already shown — we know he must fail. Calzabigi sets the scene in a 'dark labyrinthine cavern, strewn with fallen rocks and wild vegetation'. The scenery, the urgent string passage which opens the act, and the fact that the scene begins, in sharp contrast to the previous scenes, with recitative, combine to emphasise that this is a time and a place to be hurried through. All of Orpheus's words suggest movement: 'Vieni! segui i miei passi. . .meco t'affretta. . .tronchiam le dimore. . .inoltra i passi tuoi' ('Come! follow my steps. . .hurry with me. . .cut short delays. . .hasten your step').

Eurydice, waking slowly from a trance-like state, delays, questions and doubts:

Non m'abbracci? Non parli?
Guardami almen.
Dimmi, son bella ancora, qual era un dì?

Not embrace me? Not speak?
At least look at me.
Tell me, am I still as beautiful as once I was?

The tension mounts as Eurydice's pleas become ever more reasonable and Orpheus's evasions wilder and less credible. The recitative ends with Orpheus's repeated injunction, 'Ma vieni e taci! ('Come, and be silent!') – a poignant contrast to the moment in the first act when

L'idolo del mio cor
non mi risponde.

My heart's idol
answers me not.

The vigorous duet which follows has been criticised for depicting a Eurydice unworthy of Orpheus's heroism. Even Alfred Einstein, one of the most sensitive critics of Gluck's operas, wrote: 'We have to resign ourselves to the fact that Calzabigi and Gluck saw their heroine as by no means an "ideal" spouse, but quite realistically as a violent one, full of passion and blinded by jealousy' (Einstein, *Gluck,* p. 77). 'Realistic' – yes: realism is what the opera is about. But no more violent, passionate and jealous than is necessary to bring about the catastrophe. A sweetly docile Eurydice would have deprived Jove's test of its point, and her obedience to Orpheus's injunctions would have brought about a remarkably feeble ending to the drama. Eurydice's passion – and she is very passionate in both the duet and the following aria – shows the intensity of her love for Orpheus, and measures up to the violence of his grief in the first act. *Orfeo* is a supremely balanced work.

Inevitably Orpheus succumbs. Eurydice, either through a trick or through genuine emotion, feels faint. Her husband turns to her, and in a moment she is dead. Orpheus tries to revive her ('shaking her', directs Calzabigi) and calls her name repeatedly. But the wheel has turned full circle and 'la chiamo in van!' ('I call her in vain!'). He echoes Cupid's words in Act I: 'La perdo, e di nuovo, e per sempre' ('I lose her, once more, and for ever') and breaks into the musical climax of the opera, the aria 'Che farò senza Euridice?' ('What shall I do without Eurydice?').

Writing in 1770 after perhaps a dozen performances of the opera, Gluck declared:

Little or nothing but a slight alteration in the manner of expression is necessary to turn my aria in *Orfeo* 'Che farò senza Euridice?' into a puppet dance. One note held too long or too short, a careless increase in tempo or volume, one appoggiatura misplaced, an ornament, passage or roulade can ruin a whole scene in such an opera.

(Preface to *Paride ed Elena*)

'Che farò', along with the Furies' scene, was parodied in several eighteenth-century comic operas; notably, Traetta's *Il cavaliere errante* parodies the aria, and Paisiello's *Socrate immaginario* the underworld scene. If 'Che farò' is at risk, it is because of its simplicity. Like 'Chiamo il mio ben così' in Act I, and 'Deh! placatevi con me' in II. 1, it distances Orpheus's emotions, and contains them within a musical form and language of deceptive accessibility. In spite of the detailed tempo and dynamic marks in the printed score, much of its impact depends on the singer's interpretation. Anna Amalie Abert has pointed out (preface to the 1963 edition) that from beginning life as a protest against the domination and abuses of singers, *Orfeo* rapidly became a singer's opera, and spread across Europe largely through the enthusiasm of those who undertook the title role.

Inconsolable, Orpheus prepares to kill himself, but is interrupted by Cupid, who declares that Orpheus has amply demonstrated the power of love (was Jove's test, then, simply a contest between the gods?) – 'assai per gloria mia soffristi' ('you have suffered enough for my glory'). Eurydice is restored to him. Cupid cuts short their raptures and leads them to the Temple of Love, where an abundance of dancing and triumphant singing celebrates the 'bondage which is sweeter than freedom'.

The happy ending has been much criticised. Most commentators dismiss it as a consequence of the occasional nature of the first performance: 'Let not the date of the first performance of *Orfeo*, 5th October 1762, be forgotten. It was the name-day of the Emperor Francis, a day on which it would have been impossible to produce a piece with a tragic ending' (Einstein, *Gluck*, p. 70). (Heartz, 'From Garrick to Gluck', p. 122, points out that it was also the birthday of Diderot, the champion of enlightened rationalism!) But *Orfeo* was not an occasional work. Planned and written many months before the date of the première was decided, *Orfeo* was given at least two private performances in Calzabigi's house on 8 July and 6 August 1762. Neither occasion appears to have produced any criticism of the ending, and there is no evidence that any alternative to the *lieto fine* had ever been suggested by either librettist or composer.

When Calzabigi planned the ending he was no doubt influenced by those considerations of form and balance which we have observed

throughout the opera. Cupid intervenes symmetrically at the end of Act
I and of Act III. Moreover, it is a mistake to think that the happy ending
alone transforms a realistic story into a supernatural farce. The *plot* of
Orfeo does not attempt to be realistic. A story dealing with the bringing
back from the dead cannot be dealt with in other than supernatural
terms, and it is no more artificial for Cupid to revive Eurydice in the
third act than it was for him to assist Orpheus in Act I and for Orpheus
to enter the underworld in Act II. The myth of Orpheus remains a
myth, and we must not expect the plot to move on the everyday plane
of contemporary comic opera, however realistic its characters seem. It
is, of course, a tribute to the living intensity the poet and composer
have given to the characters in *Orfeo* that the 'magic' ending has attracted so much criticism. For while the plot of *Orfeo* does not pretend
to be realistic, the feelings of the protagonists do. The emotions undergone by Orpheus and Eurydice are the *raison d'être* of the opera. For
this reason, Orpheus is not punished by the Maenads or compensated
with immortality. He is above all a husband, Eurydice a wife. The only
appropriate conclusion to their reunion is an earthly marriage.

> Se foste amanti,
> conoscerete a prova
> quel focoso desio
> che mi tormenta
> che per tutto è con me.

4 'The most moving act in all opera'

BY PATRICIA HOWARD

In an important and perceptive essay included in the 1969 Decca recording, Arthur Hutchings discusses 'Romain Rolland's enormous claim that the second act of Gluck's *Orfeo* is "the most moving act in all opera" ' ('Gluck and Reform Opera', Decca (London, 1970)). The claim is a challenge. It sends us off immediately in search of all the expressive high points in opera, and dares us to compare them with the second act of *Orfeo*. More moving than Dido's lament? Than the Countess in *Figaro?* Than Isolde? Than Peter Grimes? It was not, perhaps, meant to be an exact statement about Gluck's superiority, but an incitement to take a fresh look at an old opera.

Professor Hutchings is right to direct our attention to the middle act. In a poor production, the first act of *Orfeo* can become cold and stiff, and the last act, if badly sung, tedious. But the second act never fails to make an impression, even when both the performance and the production are sub-standard. Its effect, as Rolland goes on to suggest, lies in its simplicity: the apposition of the Furies' unrelievedly sombre cavern with the serene splendour of the Elysian fields. This was Calzabigi's masterstroke, and Gluck responded with music that portrays darkness and light with a degree of effectiveness which is almost visual. The beauties of Act II are not, though, exclusively scenic. There is a figure in the landscape. The choruses of Furies and Blessed Spirits give a voice to each vista, but the human interest is focused on Orpheus, and on his reactions to the contrasted scenes. For this reason I am going to discuss only the original Vienna score of the opera in this chapter. The introduction in Act II scene 2 of *Orphée* of Eurydice, in an air ('Cet asile aimable') which is merely pastoral, disturbs the numinous atmosphere created by 'Che puro ciel' and 'Vieni a' regni' and destroys the drastic simplicity of the original plan for the act. No wonder the Parisian critic (see below, p. 73) compared this interpolation unfavourably with Rameau, and found that it 'lacks an extra nuance'. It is interesting to observe that in this act, far from being new or revolutionary, Gluck betrays an old-fashioned baroque attitude to the expression of emotion. Baroque aesthetic theory – and very largely baroque practice too – decreed that a single movement should express a single emotion, and favoured just that sharp juxtaposition of contrasting moods between movements which we find between scenes in this act. Where Gluck is innovatory, however, is in sustaining his single mood during so long a period of time: Act II scene 1 lasts for nearly three hundred bars of continuous music, and although the emotions run from despair to victory, the mood is consistently dark.

It is the unity of this scene, then, that first needs explaining. How does Gluck weld the diverse elements of chorus, dance and solo into a single musical structure? Italian opera before Gluck had consisted of a string of single numbers with no particular linking factor between them. But a mere glance at the numbers of Act II scene 1 reveals some very obvious links, and closer study discovers more (table 1).

Table 1
Act II scene 1

No.	Genre	Time signature	Key	Open-ended?
1	Ballet	¢	Eb major – C minor	yes
2	Harp passage	C	C minor	yes
3	Chorus	3/4	C minor	yes
4	Ballet	3/4	C minor	yes
5	Chorus	3/4	C minor	yes
6	Ballet	¢	Eb major – C minor	yes
7	Harp passage	¢	C minor	yes
8	Air and Chorus	¢	Eb major	no
9	Chorus	3/4	Eb major – F minor	no
10	Air	¢	F minor – C minor	no
11	Chorus	3/4	F minor	yes
12	Air	C	F minor	no
13	Chorus	3/4	F minor	no

Continuity was self-evidently a priority with Gluck. Eight of the thirteen numbers are open-ended, that is, they finish on an imperfect cadence, or pass even more imperceptibly into the following number. The main key centres of aggression (C minor) and appeasement (F minor — the same tension-lowering use of the subdominant occurs in the first act: see below, p. 74) are spaced out by the use of E flat major. Gluck's use of this major key is interesting. In the opening ballet — which returns immediately before Orpheus's first air — the music establishes the intrinsic character of the Furies: terror and torment are part of their landscape before Orpheus comes on the scene, but there is also a certain nobility, I think, expressed in the firm unisons and sweeping arpeggios (Ex. 1). Orpheus sings his first air in the same key and it has a similar dignity and detached poise. The singer seems quite impervious

Ex. 1

to the choral interruptions (Ex. 2). My guess is that Gluck intended this relatively neutral key to express the premises of the argument between Orpheus and the Furies. Its appearance at the beginning of the act establishes the nature of the opposition, and its central reappearance separates the unrelenting Fury choruses from their first expressions of

bar — ba-ro   do — lor

Ex. 2

pity and their gradual submission to the power of Orpheus's pleading.

Tonality is Gluck's principal unifying device. He was concerned not only to unify but to distinguish. A glance at the time signatures in table 1 will show that Gluck established a contrasting metrical character for each side in the conflict. All Orpheus's songs are made to seem continuous by their use of C or ¢ time, whereas the Furies' music, apart from the introductory ballet and its repeat, is in triple time. The Furies' choruses are, indeed, linked not just by metre but by the constant reiteration of the rhythmic pattern ♩ ♩ ♩ | ♩. ♪♪ (which is sung no fewer than fifty-two times, or 104 bars in a total of 149 comprising the Fury choruses). There are also melodic connections. There is much literal repetition: the first ten bars of no. 5 in table 1 are identical with no. 3, and no. 13 makes extensive use of no. 11. We can also trace a growth of melodic range and textural complexity in these choruses: the first (unison) choruses have a melodic line which keeps turning back on itself, homing on C or G (Ex. 3, from no. 3). In the later choruses, the

Chi mai del   l'E - re-bo   fral-le   ca - li - gi-ni   sul-l'or-me

d'Er - co-le   e   di   Pi - ri - to-o   con-du-ce il   piè?

Ex. 3

greater responsiveness of the Furies is expressed by rising phrases which move away from the tonics and dominants which obsess Ex. 3. The line spans a fourth, and the lower voices move independently (Ex. 4, from no. 9). This idea is expanded further when the gates are finally flung open. Gluck depicts this thrilling moment in a rising scale of immense

Ex. 4

power, mirrored by a mighty bass line in contrary motion (Ex. 5, from
no. 13). This passage typifies the extreme simplicity of Gluck's most
effective musical ideas. What more elementary device could illustrate
an opening pathway?

Ex. 5

The remarkable unity of the Fury choruses may be explained by a
number which Gluck introduced into the Paris score. (The pre-existence
of this number shows how he might well have had the melodic and
rhythmic ideas, which stamp the Fury music so unmistakably, running
through his head before he began to write *Orfeo*.) In *Orphée*, Gluck in-

serted a redundant dance movement at the end of the scene, to follow
no. 13, and this dance was taken from the score of *Don Juan,* composed
in the year before *Orfeo,* 1761. It is a fine dance movement, but the
placing is absurd. The final chorus depicts the gradual withdrawal of the
pacified Furies, their earlier inflexibility calmed to a dying murmur of
submission. To bring them back in their earlier vigour and vehemence at
this point in the score was an unhappy concession of dramatic truth to
local fashion. (In a recent production by Scottish Opera, this dance was
placed at the opening of the scene. There is some sense in this, but I
was surprised to find how much the scene lacked its epic dimensions
when the grandeur of the E flat major ballet was missing.) However, the
dance movement clearly reveals the underlying connections between
the Fury choruses and the Fury dance (no. 4 in table 1) (Ex. 6).

Ex. 6

Gluck conceived his orchestration on simple, baroque lines. Each instrument has an illustrative character and is, on the whole, restricted to this function. In Act II scene 1 Orpheus's lyre is portrayed with an unsophisticated directness by the back-stage orchestra of harp, pizzicato strings and continuo. To contrast with this, the Furies are given a fuller accompaniment of strings and continuo reinforced by oboes, cornetti, horns and trombones. These wind instruments are, however, used with considerable restraint – and perhaps considerable double-handedness among the orchestral musicians: it is possible for the horns and cornetti to be played by the same musicians throughout the opera, and this would explain some of the extremely selective scoring. (On the other hand, the question, who played the chalumeau in Act I? is not so immediately solvable – neither the flautists nor the oboists, assuming the latter doubled on cor anglais, were free to do so.) The trombones are used only to support the Furies' cries of 'No!' in no. 8, the horns appear nowhere except in the ballet (nos. 1 and 6), and the cornetti reinforce the oboes in just the middle choruses (nos. 8, 9 and 11). The fact that the Furies are elsewhere supported only by oboes, strings and

Ex. 7

continuo does not weaken the impact of their music. Gluck makes his effects more than adequately by exploiting the relentless rhythms and varying the vocal range and texture. Such modest orchestral require-

Ex. 8

ments, though, underline the chamber character of the work in its original version. An expansion of forces was necessary for Paris.

Scene 2, however, contains one of the most complex orchestral textures Gluck ever created. After the serene ballet for flutes and strings, which remains one of Gluck's best-loved creations, follows 'Che puro ciel' — accompanied recitative, *scena,* tone-poem? Gluck did not assign a genre to this unique movement: it is genuinely *sui generis* (Ex. 7). Superb as this musical portrayal of paradise is, it is perhaps even more remarkable in the context of its musical provenance. Gluck first conceived the raw material in an aria in Act I of *Ezio* (1750) which contains the melodic line (played on its first appearance, as in *Orfeo,* by an oboe and later given to a soprano voice) and the first violins' accompanying figure. There is, however, nothing in the *Ezio* aria, nor in the second working of this material in *Antigono* (1756), to suggest the subtlety of Gluck's orchestration in Act II of *Orfeo* (Ex. 8). The thrilling quality of sound in 'Che puro ciel' derives in part from the extensive use of solo instruments — flute, oboe, bassoon (now released from the continuo group), horn and cello. The motifs they play are commonplaces of eighteenth-century nature imagery — the flowing stream, the piping birdsong; many composers used similar melodic figures, but Gluck combines these fragments in a texture which is richer than anything he had ever written before, and makes what is essentially accompaniment material take the foreground, while the voice, in an unassertively low register, comments on the scene.

The overall scheme of scene 2 is even simpler than that of scene 1 (table 2). None of the numbers is open-ended, though nos. 2 and 5 end

Table 2
Act II scene 2

No.	Genre	Time signature	Key
1	Ballet	$\frac{3}{4}$	F major
2	Accompanied recitative and Chorus	C	C major
3	Chorus	$\frac{3}{8}$	F major
4	Ballet	$\frac{3}{4}$	B♭ major
5	Recitative and Chorus	C	G minor – C major
6	Chorus	$\frac{3}{8}$	F major

Ex. 9

with choral interjections which lead into the chorus 'Vieni a' regni'. F major is the basic key centre, with a move to the brighter dominant key for 'Che puro ciel' (no. 2) and a brief relaxation of tension in the subdominant ballet which separates the choruses. Gluck has retained the apposition of common and triple time to distinguish Orpheus from the chorus, though this contrast is not nearly as conspicuous as in scene 1, since Orpheus sings no aria in this scene.

After 'Che puro ciel', all the music which follows is something of an anticlimax. And yet the repeated choruses (nos. 3 and 6) are masterpieces of musical expression, too (Ex. 9). The first five-bar phrase seems to express, by its extra bar, the (deceptive) finality of the situation: Orpheus's quest is over. As the subsequent phrases unfold, each one seems perfectly matched by music which celebrates in turn both the 'great hero' and 'tender spouse', and the resurrection of Eurydice, vulnerable and fated. In his preface to the later opera *Paride ed Elena*, Gluck was to boast that he had solved the problem of depicting different races in contrasted musical styles. But already in *Orfeo* he had accomplished much more. In finding a fitting music to express the extremes of darkness and light, music which evokes the tortured and the blessed as vividly for us today as it did for the first audience two hundred years ago, Gluck arrived at a musical style which 'embraces the whole universe of passions' (letter to La Harpe, *Journal de Paris*, 12 October 1777).

5 The initial impact

First performance: documentary
BY HANS HEIMLER

The following two extracts from the *Wienerisches Diarium*, the official Viennese newspaper of the period, refer to the first performance of Gluck's *Orfeo* at the old Burgtheater. This smallish theatre, in which works like Mozart's *Figaro* and Beethoven's *Leonore/Fidelio* and his music to *Egmont* were to be performed for the first time, was demolished and replaced a century after Gluck's death by the new Burgtheater (for drama) and the Hoftheater (now the Staatsoper). Both are situated on the Ringstrasse, the essential feature of the reshaping of the inner city of Vienna under the Emperor Francis Joseph.

The short notice in the Court Diary of 6 October 1762 speaks for itself. The lengthy review of the first performance, dated 13 October, is another matter. It is rather hastily written (e.g. the sentence 'Orpheus looks back, sees his wife and she dies. . .' is repeated in two consecutive paragraphs) in a somewhat stilted German by an anonymous critic who, by implication, modestly disclaims knowledge of music ('appraisal does not depend on the often hasty utterances of amateurs'). One is led to assume that he was a court or government official with literary interests. Most of the review is concerned with Calzabigi's contribution, and it completely fails to appreciate Gluck's fundamental role in the creation of the first reform opera. The reviewer intelligently recognises the novel musico-dramatic features of the work, and attributes them exclusively to Calzabigi. The music, much to our disappointment, is summarily dealt with in half a paragraph, the other half of which concerns the choreographer. Performers are not mentioned, and only the scene-painter is criticised for not doing full justice to Quaglio's design.

Wienerisches Diarium No. 80, 6 October 1762

Last night a musical drama with the title *Orpheus and Eurydice* was performed in the theatre near the Imperial Palace (Hofburg) in the presence of the court. It was received with general acclaim and brings much honour to its author, Herr Calzabigi, and to the composer of the music, the Cav. Gluck.

Wienerisches Diarium No. 82, 13 October 1762 (Wednesday supplement)

On the fifth of this month the new Italian opera (Singspiel) *Orpheus and Eurydice* was given for the first time here in Vienna at the theatre near the Imperial Palace (Hofburg) in the presence of the imperial and royal court. In describing this opera with the first expression that comes to mind when sympathetically judging our stage performances, one would declare this a successful piece that was received with extraordinary acclaim. None the less, appraisal of its inner worth does not depend on the often hasty utterances of amateurs, but rather on the strict opinions of the experts in singing poesy (Dichtkunst). The latter have pronounced it beautiful and the invention and execution excellent. They knew in advance the merits of its author, Herr Ranerius v. Calzabigi of Leghorn, imperial and royal titulary councillor at the Netherlands Chamber of Finance, who has published in France a new edition of the works of Abate [sic] Metastasio, and attracted the attention of scholars by his beautiful introduction to this collection. He has also proved his philosophical insight into poetry in other contexts.

Despite poetical elaboration, the legend of Orpheus and Eurydice remains recognisable right to the end, and it has lost nothing of beauty in the hands of our poet. He has introduced some changes, but how reasonably! They are really embellishments and must be accepted as decisive features that indicate the hand of the master. The disposition is new and the coherence natural. Tenderness and the miraculous predominate, expressed with economy by the language of tender passion, without superfluous frills. Let us follow the author back to his first outline.

Orpheus weeps over the loss of his beloved Eurydice. The gods hear his lament. The god of love conveys to him their permission to bring Eurydice back from the underworld. The command not to look at her before their arrival in the upper regions is familiar from the legend, but the order to keep this prohibition secret is a fruitful invention by the author. The gentle Orpheus is confident of his strength to fulfil both these conditions. He overcomes all obstacles and finds the animated shade of his wife. With his face averted, he leads her towards the realms of the upper world. His refusal to look back is bound to appear strange to her, and when she asks for a reason, she is told to follow him with faster steps. The tenderest husband is bound to arouse suspicions under these circumstances. Eurydice weeps, she reproaches him, death seems preferable to her. Grief is too strong for her heart and she sinks down. . . To keep a secret is not the most difficult task for a reasonable man, but not to give help to a suffering wife is asking too much of a husband whose resolve has been weakened. Orpheus looks back, sees his wife and she dies. . .

The author deserves our thanks for not showing us Orpheus in the hateful image of a man who, because of impertinence or mistrust in the gods, has received the just punishment of losing a lovable wife for ever. He has instead portrayed a tender husband and made us witness a crime whose causes are love and tenderness. Orpheus looks back, sees his wife and she dies. . .A lapse caused by love can be rectified by none better than the god of love. The poet recalls him to bring Eurydice back to life. Here too one should not misjudge the well-considered discretion used out of a pleasing regard for the requirements of our local theatre, to which he has drawn attention in his preface. Thus the tragic ending of the legend has been turned into a joyous one. All spectators, who otherwise would have returned to their homes saddened by shared suffering, are most grateful to him for this happy change. And has virtuous Orpheus, as he is shown throughout, not merited a happier fate?

We have gladly accompanied the poet through a series of changing emotional states and participated in the pleasant feelings for which he has prepared us by the poetic treatment of the legend.

The choruses, in whose reintroduction we rejoice, and the activity given to them by Herr Calzabigi show sufficiently how well he knows the traditions and customs of the classics. The apt treatment of the two singing protagonists is proportionate to the value of the opera as a whole. They proceed from [the expression of] one passion to another without the slightest deviation. The airs, mainly responsible for this, are here placed correctly where they do not interrupt the mood (Affekt) but rather express it more touchingly.

The music is by our famous Cav. Christoph Gluck who has surpassed himself in it. Perfect harmony prevails throughout; characters and passions are clearly and sensitively expressed; the feelings of the listener are constantly stimulated by a rational change of speed and a good choice and variety of instruments. Herr Casp. Angiolini has confirmed his own special skill in the elaboration of the dances by linking them to the choruses and to the legend in a way that makes them as impressive as instructive.

Herr Quaglio, who undertook the decoration of the stage, has again proved himself an inventive artist, above all in the special way in which he represents the Elysian fields. With a stage thus transformed it was impossible, even if one remained ignorant of the aim of the presentation, to expect anything other than the appearance of the blessed shades of dead heroes. The design of the cave through which Orpheus leads his Eurydice to the upper regions is indeed beautiful, but we can not convince ourselves that the brush of the painter has carried out the true intentions of the designer.

The text of the opera has been translated into German by Herr Jac. Ant. Edler von Ghelen, whose pen is already known through similar work.

First performance: speculation
BY PATRICIA HOWARD

The account in the *Wienerisches Diarium* tells us everything about the first performance of *Orfeo* except those things we would most like to know. And yet it is the only source actually to describe, albeit in a limited way, the performances on 5 and 10 October 1762. The criticism of the work in the unpublished diaries of Count Zinzendorf (quoted in Haas, *Gluck und Durazzo*, p. 62) relates chiefly to Calzabigi's poem, and constitutes an invalid attack on the poet's neglect of the classical unities. And no musician seems to have taken up a pen in delight at or disapproval of this historic event.

We are indebted to the libretti for the cast-list of those performances:
Orfeo: Gaetano Guadagni
Euridice: Marianna Bianchi
Amor: Lucia Clavarau

But the libretti which give us this information pose further questions which no complementary source has yet answered. Libretti in the eighteenth century fulfilled many of the functions of programmes today. They were 'normally published afresh with each production, and contained information about the performers and the performance which is unobtainable elsewhere. There exist two libretti from the year 1762, both of which contain the above cast-list. One is printed by Jean Thomas Trattner and gives the text on alternate pages in Italian and French. The other, published by von Ghelen, gives the Italian text only. However, neither of these dates from the first performance, for the anonymous Court Diarist notes that 'the text of the opera has been translated into German by Herr Jac. Ant. Edler von Ghelen' – implying that a bilingual libretto in Italian and German was issued to accompany the performance he is reviewing.

The first production was repeated in the same year on 10 and 21 October and 9 and 12 December, and in 1763 on 13 February and 24 and 25 July.

Compared with the detailed accounts of the preparations associated with Gluck's reworking of *Orfeo* for Paris in 1774, we know little of the activities of 1762. It is probable that Calzabigi brought the poem with him when he came to Vienna from Paris in 1761, that Durazzo introduced him to Gluck in the same year and that the composition began early in 1762. The score was completed by the summer. After the fashion of the time, the work was introduced to a small circle of sympathetic connoisseurs in private performances on 8 July and 6 August. Count Zinzendorf (quoted in Haas, *Gluck und Durazzo,* p. 62) tells us that both previews were held at Calzabigi's house with Guadagni singing his part and Gluck at the harpsichord supplying everything else. (Gluck introduced *Orphée* to Paris in exactly similar circumstances: see below, p. 71).

Rehearsals at the Burgtheater must have followed in early autumn. The only account we have of these comes from Gluck's reminiscences to Dr Burney, some ten years later:

Gluck recounted to me the difficulties he had met with in disciplining the band, both of vocal and instrumental performers, at the rehearsals of *Orfeo,* which was the first of his operas that was truly dramatic. . . He is a great disciplinarian, and as formidable as Handel used to be, when at the head of a band; but he assured me, that he never found his troops mutinous, though he, on no account, suffered them to leave any part of their business, till it was well done, and frequently obliged them to repeat some of his manoeuvres twenty or thirty times.

(Burney, *Music in Germany,* pp. 99, 117)

Burney draws the comparison between Gluck and Handel. We might add Lully who, a hundred years earlier, was also trying to sweep away the accretions of tradition and to impose a new precision on singers and players alike, gaining a similar reputation for severity. There are no stories of Gluck breaking a violin over the head of an offending player as Lully did, nor of him threatening, like Handel, to throw his *prima donna* out of the window, but he was, Burney assures us, 'a very dragon, of whom all are in fear' (*ibid.* p. 89).

In spite of these tantalising hints, there are no descriptions of the musical qualities of the early performances. It seems obvious to us that the whole success of the opera depended on Guadagni, and yet no account of Guadagni's interpretation of the role has come down to us. As we have already noted, Guadagni was Garrick-trained, and apparently sought to achieve his effects by acting rather than vocal embellishment. The lack of ornamentation in *Orfeo* must have been novel to be considered worthy of mention by Burney: 'The chevalier Gluck is simplifying music. . .he tries all he can to keep his music chaste and sober. His three operas of *Orfeo, Alceste,* and *Paride,* are proofs of this, as they contain few difficulties of execution, though many of expression' (*ibid.* p. 83). There is evidence, though, which suggests that Gluck's 'simplification' was only relative. The composer and singing master Domenico Corri published in 1779 *A Select Collection of the Most Admired Songs, Duetts etc. from Operas in the Highest Esteem.* In this volume he includes three arias from *Orfeo,* 'Che farò', 'Chiamo il mio ben così' and 'Deh! placatevi'. Each number is headed 'composed by M. Gluck. Sung by Sigr. Guadagni' and is written out with detailed though modest ornamentation, breathing marks (where, Corri tells us, a slight pause is to be made) and the occasional cadenza. The reprise of 'Che farò' indicates the degree of embellishment in this volume (Ex. 10).

Ex. 10   From *A Select Collection of the Most Admired Songs, Duetts etc. from Operas in the Highest Esteem,* ed. Domenico Corri (London, 1779), pp. 38-43. The aria is headed 'Composed by M. Gluck. Sung by Sigr. Guadagni.'

Now Corri's *Collection* sets out to define the taste of the age. He does not head the arias '*as* sung by Sigr. Guadagni', and this ornamentation may have nothing to do with the way the role of Orpheus was performed in 1762. In a companion volume to the *Collection,* a teaching manual called *The Singer's Preceptor,* Corri advocates restrained ornamentation, and associates this style of singing with, if not Guadagni, at least the second exponent of the Orpheus role, Giuseppe Millico:

> Those famous singers Farinelli, Cafarello, Geziello, Pachiarotti [who sang Orpheus at Naples in 1774], Milico, Aprili, David, Raff, and others of the first eminence, sung compositions with little ornament, exerting their talents, on the parts appointed to them; nor were they permitted to introduce, at random, any graces, ornaments etc. as caprice directed; but in such places only as the composer had allotted. . .Their merit consisted in the Portamento di voce. . .Portamento di voce is the perfection of vocal music; it consists in the swell and dying of the voice, the sliding and blending one note into another with delicacy and expression – and expression comprehends every charm which music can produce. . .
>
> Words either in speaking or singing have most effect when accompanied with suitable expression of countenance, as described in these elegant lines of the Rt. Hon. R. B. Sheridan:
>
>> Sheridan's Monody on Garrick's Death
>> 'The Grace of Action – the adapted Mien
>> Faithful as Nature to the varied scene;
>> Th'expressive Glance – whose subtle comment draws
>> Entranc'd attention, and a mute applause;
>> Gesture that marks, with force and feeling fraught,
>> A sense in Silence, and a will in Thought.'
>
> (*The Singer's Preceptor,* pp. 3-4)

It is fascinating to observe that Corri harks back to Garrick, the touchstone of all that was held to be admirable in mid-eighteenth-century theatrical performances.

Guadagni performed the role in London in 1770 and 1771, where Burney commended his 'attitudes, action, and impassioned and exquisite manner of singing the simple and ballad-like air: *Che farò'* (*General History,* II, p. 877). He also sang it in Munich in 1773 and in Padua in the 1780s. Michael Kelly describes a visit to the ageing celebrity:

> Padua was interesting to me, as the birth-place of Tartini, and the two greatest singers of their time were living there retired, Pacchierotti and Guadagni. The latter was a Cavaliere. He had built a house, or rather a palace, in which he had a very neat theatre, and a company of puppets, which represented L'Orpheo e Euridice; himself singing the part of Orpheo behind the scenes. It was in this character, and in singing Gluck's beautiful rondo in it, 'Che farò senza Euridice,' that he distinguished himself in every theatre in Europe, and drew such immense houses in London.
>
> (*Reminiscences,* p. 151)

So Gluck's apprehension that 'Che farò' might one day turn into a puppet dance was realised! Guadagni was one of the foremost singers in eighteenth-century Europe. His performances were universally praised and widely described. And yet we shall never know what were the notes he actually sang in Gluck's great role.

The diffusion through Europe
BY EVE BARSHAM

The popularity of *Orfeo* on the continent dates from the successful première of the next reform opera, *Alceste*. From 1767 onwards, a growing list of performances is recorded in a widening area which before the end of the eighteenth century had extended from Spain to Stockholm and from Dublin to Budapest, as is shown by the following list of productions of *Orfeo* in Europe in the eighteenth and early nineteenth centuries:

1769	Parma (under Gluck's direction)
1770	London; Breslau
1771	Florence; Bologna; London
1773	Munich; Stockholm; Florence; London
1774	Naples; Budapest; Paris, in the new French version (this version (see Chapter 6) was given almost continuously in Paris during the eighteenth century, the only significant gap being between 1784 and 1789 when there seem to have been no performances)
1776	Brussels; Hamburg; Warsaw; Esterháza (conducted by Haydn)
1779	Brno; The Hague; Copenhagen
1780	Copenhagen; Barcelona
1781	Vienna (the French version was given in June and the Italian version (but with Orpheus sung by a tenor) in December)
1782	St Petersburg; Padua; Mainz
1783	Lille; Frankfurt; Hanover
1784	Dublin; Padua
1785	London
1786	Salzburg; Stockholm
1787	Kassel
1788	Bologna
1789	Warsaw
1790	Avignon
1792	London
1794	Charleston, S.C. (probably Gluck's opera; the performance was billed as '*Orphée* by Paisielo', but Paisiello did not write an opera of that title and the work given is now thought to

have been Gluck's French score)

1795	Siena
1799	Madrid
1801	Lisbon
1804	Clausenberg
1806	Brunswick
1808	Berlin; Brescia
1813	Milan (with Demoiselle Fabre as Orpheus – probably the first appearance of a female singer in the role)
1818	Berlin
1821	Berlin
1838	Dresden
1841	Berlin

The slow acceptance of Gluck's opera in Vienna, its city of origin, was succeeded by total neglect there after the performances in 1781, and it was not revived until the centenary production in 1862. But, in contrast, the performances in six Italian cities are evidence of an unprecedented success for any *opera seria* written by a foreigner and premièred outside Italy. The absence of any performances at Venice, a major operatic centre, is notable. It can probably be ascribed to the production there in 1776 of Bertoni's setting of Calzabigi's text. Bertoni is now best remembered as the composer who attempted to pass off as his own an aria of Gluck's used for the last number in Act I of *Orphée*. Bertoni, in the preface to his own opera, admits his general indebtedness to Gluck, and the authorship of this particular aria was a matter of dispute for nearly a hundred years (see below, pp. 82 and 109-12). Bertoni's *Orfeo* achieved publication and widespread performance in Europe, and Guadagni sang the role of Orpheus in both the operas.

The first staging of the opera with German words took place in Brno, the capital of Moravia, in 1779 under the direction of Johann Böhm who, during the 1780s, directed further performances in various German towns, his wife singing the part of Eurydice and his daughter, Nanette, that of Amor (Cupid). History was to repeat itself for her a few years later when, after her marriage to a ballet-master of this name, she became Mrs Amor in real life! Stockholm proved to be the first Scandinavian city to stage a performance of *Orfeo*, in 1773. Interestingly, this was in a version with the role of Orpheus sung by a tenor, a year before Gluck himself made a similar adaptation for Paris. In 1786 a Swedish version was made, and Gluck's operas were soon performed there on a regular basis. The Danes were less welcoming, with fewer performances in Copenhagen, possibly because of a rival setting in the Danish language by the German composer Naumann.

In operatic centres elsewhere the response was slower. There were few productions in Spain and Russia and probably none at all in Portugal before the end of the eighteenth century, while New York had to wait until 1863 to see Gluck's masterpiece. In Brussels and Warsaw it was first performed in 1776 and in the same year it was also given at Esterháza, on the Austro-Hungarian border, where Haydn worked for several decades. Earlier in the 1770s Haydn had met Gluck, and he was himself responsible for the direction of the opera at the summer palace of his patron and employer, Prince Nicholas Esterházy. The conservative musical tastes of another famous patron, Frederick the Great, ensured that Berlin was the last European operatic centre to hear *Orfeo* – it was not performed there until 1808, long after Frederick's death. During his reign, in spite of his interest in new political and philosophical theories, the old-fashioned operas of Hasse and Graun had been permitted to dominate the stage, and it is ironic that the first opera put on for Frederick William II, who succeeded him in 1786, was Bertoni's *Orfeo* – which we seem destined not to be allowed to forget. Only slowly did the Prussians learn to appreciate the reform style, though the popularity of Gluck's opera in Berlin in the nineteenth century is remarkable.

But it was in France, and especially in Paris, that Gluck's opera flourished as nowhere else in Europe. In the first seventy years of its existence, *Orphée* was given nearly three hundred times in the capital city alone. And among the audience at the performances in the 1820s was Hector Berlioz, who, in 1859, was to amalgamate the Italian and the French versions of the score and so open a new chapter in the history of its dissemination.

Orpheus in England
BY EVE BARSHAM

Among the many insignificant settings of the Orpheus story that appeared earlier in the eighteenth century had been some intended for English audiences, London having established itself as one of the principal operatic centres ever since Handel had settled there and begun his long series of productions with *Rinaldo* in 1711. Three major opera houses and several smaller establishments set up to rival each other's attractions: Italian opera was staged at the King's Theatre in the Haymarket, and the theatres in Covent Garden and Drury Lane were presenting opera in English. Naturally there was a great deal of inter-influence, passing to and fro of singers, plagiarism, satire and general intrigue.

In 1736 the 'Italian' King's Theatre staged a *pasticcio* entitled *Orfeo* by Hasse, Vinci, Araja and Porpora. A *pasticcio* (Italian for 'pie') was an entertainment which combined music by several composers, often taken from earlier works. Concocting such a hotch-potch gave less trouble than providing new material and served to attract a wider public because of the combination of talents. The success of this *Orfeo* may have been the cause of the publication of no fewer than three Orpheus libretti in 1740, a situation which brought about a flurry of pamphlets and much bad feeling between the authors. Only one of these libretti was actually set to music and staged and this, which had comic episodes, was composed by John Lampe. Undoubtedly the sensation of the piece, according to the *Memoirs* (1806) of the dramatist Richard Cumberland, was the snake which causes Eurydice's death:

Nothing could be more perfect in his entrances and exits, nothing ever crawled across the stage with more accomplished sinuosity than this enchanting serpent; every soul was charmed with its performances; it twirled and twisted and wriggled itself about in so divine a manner, the whole world was ravished with the lovely snake: nobles and non-nobles, rich and poor, old and young, reps and demi-reps flocked to see it, and admire it. The artist, who had been the master of the movement, was intoxicated with his success; he turned his hands and head to nothing else but serpents; he made them of all sizes, they crawled about his shop as if he had been chief snake-catcher to the furies: the public curiosity was satisfied with one serpent, and he had nests of them yet unsold; his stock lay dead upon his hands, his trade was lost, and the man was ruined, bankrupt and undone.

(pp. 473-4)

Gluck's *Orfeo* reached the stage of the King's Theatre only eight years after the Viennese première, surprisingly soon by English standards; Orpheus was sung by Guadagni. But this 1770 production proved to be the beginning of the progressive watering-down, *pasticcio*-fashion, of Gluck's opera in London. The work, referred to as 'opera in the Grecian taste', was lengthened with words by Giovanni Bottarelli and with music by J. C. Bach who (according to the title page of the libretto in the British Library) 'has very kindly condescended to add of his own new composition all such choruses and recitatives as are marked with inverted commas'. Guglielmi, the producer, had also added arias for his wife (playing Eurydice), and such was the quantity of additions that only seven numbers of Gluck's original score remained. A new character, Tiresia, swelled the cast when the *pasticcio* was repeated in 1771, again with Guadagni, and Londoners seemed to prefer this travesty to the real thing, if the quick dismissal of an 'original' production in 1773 and the

2   Giusto Ferdinando Tenducci, the Orfeo of pastiche versions in London between 1771 and 1785

reinstatement of the doctored version is a guide to public reaction. Parody may be seen as a kind of backhanded compliment to the success of an opera. In 1767 Garrick inserted a comic interlude, *The Burletta of Orpheus* (with music by a Frenchman, Barthélemon), into his play *A Peep behind the Curtain*. This satirises pre-reform Italian opera, and ends with a dance of shepherds, trees and cows – which latter seem to have proved an expensive item.

The serious J. C. Bach version reached Dublin in 1784 and for the first time the words were in English. There, too, we have proof of its success in a burletta by Giordani which appeared a couple of months later. Back in London, two more productions carried the opera further than ever from its origins. In 1785 Tenducci presented a version in which, he remarked in the preface, 'Besides the music of Gluck, of Bach, and of some other famous masters, there are introduced several pieces by the immortal Handel which I hope will delight much more than the many compositions which have nothing new but the name.' The final depths were reached in 1792 when an English version at the Theatre Royal, Covent Garden, was made up of music by 'Gluck, Handel, Bach, Sacchini and Weichsel with additional new Music by William Reeve'. In this version (of which Preston & Son published a vocal score), virtually nothing of the original score survived except Orpheus's famous lament, sung however with the disappointingly impersonal opening words, 'What, alas, shall Orpheus do?' After a handful of unsuccessful performances, no version of Gluck's opera was produced in London for nearly three-quarters of a century.

Meanwhile, in the early months of the previous year (1791), Haydn, on a visit to London, was writing his final opera, *L'anima del filosofo o sia Orfeo e Euridice*, an *opera seria* in four acts with a libretto by Badini. Haydn was most enthusiastic about this opera, and wrote to Prince Anton Esterházy on 8 January:

The new opera libretto which I am to compose is entitled *Orfeo*, in 5 acts [*sic*], but I shall not receive it for a few days. It is supposed to be entirely different from that of Gluck. The prima donna is called Madame Lops from Munich. . .Seconda donna is Madame Capelletti. Primo homo is the celebrated Davide. . .the opera is supposed to contain many choruses, ballets and a lot of big changes of scenery.

> (Quoted in H. C. Robbins Landon, *Haydn in England*
> (London, 1976), p. 38)

Described by Robbins Landon (*ibid.* p. 351) as 'basically a magnificent failure', the opera was not performed in its entirety until 1951 (in Florence, with a cast which included Boris Christoff and Maria Callas).

Its 'failure' probably results from both the librettist's and the composer's insufficiently dramatic treatment of Eurydice's second death, and the 'age of reason' style of the neo-Metastasian libretto in which a major character, King Creonte (the father of Eurydice), philosophises in a manner more suited to oratorio than opera. The cast is much larger than Gluck's, containing four major singing parts and seven minor roles. The chorus also takes a more active part, both participating in the action and reflecting on it in the Greek manner. The story, following Ovid, does not end with Eurydice's restoration to life and to her husband, but with Orpheus's destruction by the Bacchae and the final floating away of his body towards the isle of Lesbos as a storm arises on the river Lethe. Haydn's opera was never staged in his lifetime. Perhaps pastiches of Gluck's work had sated the London audiences' taste for mythology and miracles – with or without serpents.

6 From 'Orfeo' to 'Orphée'

BY PATRICIA HOWARD

From revolutionary to conservative

When Gluck revised *Orfeo* for the Paris stage in 1774, he was acting not through any dissatisfaction with his original score, but in an attempt to fit the work to the local taste. It was a move in a carefully planned campaign to conquer the French operatic world, and, as Gluck himself declared, to break down the divisions and prejudices which had held sway for a hundred years – divisions which had attempted to isolate the French capital from the near-universal style of Italian opera, and prejudices, for and against French opera, which had generated much critical heat in the war of aesthetics raging throughout the century.

Why should Gluck have wanted to conquer Paris? His attitude to composition is as little documented as that of any eighteenth-century composer. As we have seen, he seems to have been led into the reform of opera by those more aware of contemporary trends. But having stumbled on the dramatic truth of *Orfeo,* he built *Alceste* consciously upon the same principles, and by the time he had completed the third reform opera, *Paride ed Elena* (1769), he was bemoaning the lack of 'imitators, who, encouraged by the full support of an enlightened public, would follow the new path' (preface to *Paride ed Elena*). Paris must have seemed to offer a more fruitful artistic climate for the 'new path'. His reform operas already met the French taste halfway, and it was not by chance that the score of *Orfeo* was first published in Paris rather than in Vienna. So for a decade Gluck devoted himself to French opera, writing new works (perhaps his finest) in the tradition of *tragédie lyrique* invented by Lully and developed by Rameau, and 'translating' two of his Italian operas into the same idiom.

Gluck's strategy was first to secure influential patronage. The arrival in Paris in June 1772 of his former singing pupil, the Dauphine Marie Antoinette, may have seemed opportune. It was certainly in that same year that he first made contact with a French nobleman, the Bailly du Roullet, an attaché at the French Embassy in Vienna. And within a few months, Gluck was not only working on a new opera with a libretto by du Roullet *(Iphigénie en Aulide)*, but was also opening a correspondence in the *Mercure de France* which attempted to disarm attacks from both the pro-French and the pro-Italian sides in the critical war: 'I have found a musical language fit for all nations, and hope to abolish the ridiculous distinctions between national styles of music' *(Mercure de France*, 1 February 1773). At about this time, too, Gluck must have renewed contact with the librettist Pierre-Louis Moline. They had already collaborated on the *opéra-comique L'arbre enchanté* (1759), and it was Moline who had supplied a French prose translation of Calzabigi's *Orfeo* when the score was published in Paris in 1764. Gluck now engaged Moline to translate Calzabigi's libretto into verse, and to reshape the Italian opera for the French stage. The première of *Iphigénie* was on 19 April 1774 and the work took Paris by storm. As soon as possible after this event (the theatre was closed from 1 May to 15 June during the illness of the king) Gluck presented the revised opera *Orphée et Euridice*. The première was on 2 August 1774 and the score was published almost immediately.

Orphée had an even more resounding success than *Iphigénie*. During the last five months of the year forty-seven performances were given, and the opera continued to feature prominently in the repertoire during the last decades of the century, throughout the Terror, and well into the nineteenth century, when Berlioz fell under the spell of admittedly far from authentic performances. That *Orphée* was more immediately successful in Paris than *Orfeo* had been in Vienna was due in part to the conservative nature of Parisian opera-going: long runs of a single opera had been imposed on the public during Lully's monopoly of opera performance in the seventeenth century, and the custom lingered into the eighteenth century, contributing, no doubt, to the financial stability of the Académie Royale. But the acclaim which greeted *Orphée,* and the enduring affection in which it was held, also reflect the different status of the French version. *Orfeo* was a revolutionary work, in a genre almost without precedent, designed to provoke thought and further experiment rather than repeated hearings. *Orphée,* in spite of Gluck's talk of an international musical style, was tailored so precisely to French taste and fashion that it became a highly conservative work, reinforcing the regular audience in their cherished prejudices, and wooing rather than provoking the more thoughtful spectators.

Gluck's principal task in creating *Orphée* was to transform a short and intimate court opera – almost a chamber opera – into a full-length entertainment for a public opera house. The changes in scale between *Orfeo* and *Orphée* all derive from this necessity. The added ballets in

Acts II and III not only pandered to local tradition, but were needed to fill the larger stage and to pad out the longer duration. The extra arias added to Act I were, unlike the unassuming 'songs' of the original version, well suited to the larger auditorium; and the new controversial bravura number for Orpheus fittingly expressed those aspects of the character which the change of voice from alto castrato to tenor revealed.

Gluck at the Académie Royale

The soloists on 2 August 1774 were:

Orphée: Joseph Le Gros

Euridice: Sophie Arnould

Amour: Rosalie Levasseur

According to the libretto, the chorus numbered 20 women and 27 men. The orchestra was a large one, probably comprising 28 violins, 6 violas, 12 cellos, 5 double basses, 2 flutes, 4 oboes, 2 clarinets, 4 bassoons, 2 horns, 3 trumpets, 3 trombones, and timpani. Gluck's score also calls for a harp, which had to be engaged specially for the occasion. The omission of the less usual instruments featured in the Vienna score — cornetti, chalumeaux and cors anglais — was obviously due to their unavailability in Paris.

The most striking change in the Paris version of the opera is the remodelling of the principal role from alto castrato to tenor — or, more properly, *haute-contre*. The castrato voice, in the Italian tradition of opera prevailing at Vienna, was in many opinions the finest musical instrument of the age. The immense social and artistic prestige of the castrato made this voice the obvious choice for the god of song. It combined the most sophisticated vocal technique and range of expression with a pure and detached tone. But it is easy for us, with our twentieth-century prejudices, to make too much of this point. In mid-eighteenth-century Vienna, the castrato voice would have been considered just as suitable for a heroic role, or even that of a lover. The *haute-contre* voice was a French speciality, discovered by Lully, and cultivated by him for the heroic solo roles in his operas. It was also used for the 'contralto' line of his choruses, and its handling in this context convinces me that, in the seventeenth century at least, the voice involved a mixture of falsetto and full-voice production, a style of singing still heard in opera in Paris today. It seems likely, though, that Le Gros sang the whole role 'full voice'. The fact that tenors who succeeded him (for example Louis Nourrit) had to have parts of the role transposed downwards suggests that there was no easy option to the strenuous tessitura of the 1774 score. It is ironic that Gluck twice modelled the role of Orpheus on a type of voice no longer available to us, forcing twentieth-century conductors to use compromise versions (see Chapter 8).

3   Joseph Le Gros, the first Orphée

When Gluck recast the role for Paris (where castrati had never played a prominent part in musical traditions and where, by 1774, they were objects of ridicule), he did not deliberately alter the protagonist's character from demi-god to hero or husband. He simply exchanged the vocal ideal of one country for its equivalent in another. And in fact we can prove that Gluck viewed both the register and the voice-type of Orpheus with an amazing tolerance and flexibility. One of his earliest remodellings of the opera was the transposition of much of the Orpheus role to suit the soprano castrato Giuseppe Millico for the performance at Parma in 1769. And from that date, soprano and alto castrato performances were equally common throughout Europe – France excepted. But more surprising is the fact that when *Orphée* was in rehearsal in the summer of 1774, two private performances were given at the house of the Abbé Morellet in which the tenor role of the French score was sung by Millico (with Gluck's niece Marianne taking both Eurydice and Cupid, and with Gluck at the harpsichord). Abbé Morellet's literary lunches were attended by some of the most influential writers and musicians in France, and these two 'performances' (on 5 June and 3 July) were probably given before La Harpe, d'Alembert, Suard, Grétry, François Philidor and the Abbé Arnaud.

Soprano, alto or tenor: the evidence suggests that Gluck was far less concerned with the actual pitch and timbre of his singers' voices than with their expression and acting ability. Guadagni came to Gluck already an accomplished actor, Garrick-trained. Millico, whose acting was described by Burney as 'delicate and pathetic' (*General History*, II, p. 894), must have satisfied Gluck when he sang Orpheus at Parma, or the composer would hardly have re-engaged him to create the role of Pairs in *Paride ed Elena* in the same year. (Gluck and Millico became firm friends, and Gluck entrusted the musical education of his beloved niece to Millico's care – no small tribute to the singer's musicianship.) By contrast, Le Gros seems to have had no acting ability to speak of when Gluck began to rehearse *Orphée;* perhaps this is why Millico was given the role in the two 'previews'. Indeed, the improvement wrought in Le Gros' acting was a major talking-point in Paris: 'I declare that in considering what the role of Orpheus has done for M. Le Gros, I am tempted to believe that the chevalier Gluck's music is more stirring and theatrical than that of any other composer' (Abbé Arnaud, quoted in Le Blond, *Mémoires*, p. 50). Melchior Grimm wrote that 'it is difficult not to regard this metamorphosis [of Le Gros] as one of the most prominent miracles wrought by the enchanter Gluck' (*Correspondance littéraire* (Paris, 1774), p. 472). Contemporary reminiscences describe Gluck coaching Le Gros in the opening chorus:

> My good Sir, it is intolerable: you always scream when you should sing, and when it is a question of screaming, you don't. Think at this moment neither of the music nor of the chorus, but scream with just as much anguish as if someone were sawing through your bone. And, if you can, realise this pain inwardly, spiritually, and as if it came from the heart.
>
> (Mannlich, *Ein deutscher Maler*, p. 274)

Paris being at this time virtually synonymous with literary and aesthetic pamphleteering, there are lengthy, detailed criticisms of the opera in the *Mercure de France,* the *Journal des Beaux-Arts* and many private letters. Rousseau called the work 'epoch-making' (letter to Marin, quoted in Desnoiresterres, *Gluck et Piccinni,* p. 116), and Madame de Genlis wrote of her addiction to it, which drove her to attend every rehearsal: 'Both my passionate appetite for the music, and the great pleasure of seeing Gluck, at each and every rehearsal, lose his temper with the actors and the musicians and proceed to give them sound instruction, impels me to spend every afternoon in my box' (*Mémoires,* II, p. 264).

The initial reception was not uncritical, but was far more glowing than any press notice Gluck had previously received. The comparisons with Lully and Rameau recur in virtually every published criticism of the opera:

> the poet, constrained to adapt the French language to music designed for Italian words, could only produce feeble and often irregular verses; but he should be praised for following the phrasing and structure of the music and for 'naturalising' it for our stage.
>
> The plot is surely too simple for three acts. Its uneventfulness and monotony produce tedium. The hesitations of Orpheus and the irresolution of the lovers on leaving the underworld are conducive neither to dramatic interest nor to realism. But the music compensates for these faults. It confirms our estimate, based on *Iphigénie en Aulide,* of the genius and great talent of M. le chevalier Gluck to depict and express the heart's emotions.
>
> The overture is a fine introduction to the drama, though we found its principal motif recurs too often, creating monotony. The chorus in the funeral scene is richly and movingly written. Orpheus's cries when he calls his Eurydice have great pathos. The whole of this magnificent movement, and the touching airs which follow it, fill the mind with melancholy. Cupid's gentle and consoling songs enchant the ear. The air at the end of Act I, 'L'espoir renaît dans mon âme', could not be more brilliant, more soundly constructed, or better designed to bring out the skill of a great singer with a fine voice, such as M. Le Gros.

The infernal chorus and the famous 'Non!' of the demons produce a fine effect when set in apposition to the prayers and tender, touching songs of Orpheus, accompanied by an imitation of his lyre. There is much art in the manner in which Orpheus wins over the demons so that they voluntarily open the gates of hell for him to enter. The tranquil beauty of the Elysian fields is expressed in some degree in the sweet music of the chorus of Blessed Spirits.

The funeral scene, the depiction of hell and of the Elysian fields recall — but in no way surpass — the same tableaux similarly executed in Rameau's opera, *Castor*. We believe the French composer's music to be more deeply felt, more suitable and, as it were, more apt for the localities than that of M. le chevalier Gluck. Gluck's music is too simply pastoral: it lacks an extra nuance.

As we have said, the scene in the third act between Eurydice and Orpheus is tedious, despite the great duet which, in its animated feeling, would alone suffice to bear witness to Gluck's genius.

The recitative in this opera much resembles that of Lully, but it is like his most declamatory recitative, delivered in speech rather than in song, as became the custom after his death. The orchestral movements are well written, although they sometimes appear too complicated and are less expressive than they would be if they were built on simpler harmonies.

The dances are in general more polished and more varied than those in *Iphigénie*. Some are of an originality and piquancy that Rameau himself might envy. There are only two principal roles in this opera. Eurydice is sung and acted to perfection, with expression, meaning and accuracy, by Mlle Arnould who, in her absence, is ably replaced by Mlle Beaumesnil, a fine actress and an excellent musician. Orpheus is very well performed by M. Le Gros, who brings to a superb voice, a brilliant technique, and accurate singing, the most expressive and moving acting. Mlle Rosalie acted and sang delightfully her favourite role of Cupid. Mlle Châteauneuf has replaced her in the role and won much applause.

The ballets of the funeral scene and infernal regions are choreographed by M. Gardel; those of the Elysian fields and the Temple of Love by M. Vestris: they are a credit to both. This opera displays the fine talents of the dancers with lively effect. Mlle Guimard is an excellent dancer whose steps express grace and voluptuousness; Mlle Heinel dances with nobility and dignity; M. Vestris combines Art with Nature; M. Gardel has the boldest talent — all these are our finest dancers, while in addition the brilliant Mlle Dorival and M. Gardel junior, dancing together and separately, have drawn great approbation from a devoted public.

(*Mercure de France,* 15 September 1774)

The widespread acclaim of *Orphée* is evident in the continuity of performance, the publication of single numbers of the opera for drawing-room use, and the existence of parodies — most notably *Le petit Orphée* (1785) by J. Rouhier-Deschamps. Although *Orphée* is considerably longer than the Vienna score, it still fell short of the expected duration of a full evening's entertainment, and was usually given in combination with a ballet. The score remained remarkably intact, however, during the revivals in the eighteenth century. Most of the alterations occurred in the final scene, which had already shown pastiche elements in the score of 1774. Ludwig Finscher (in the preface to the 1967 edition) points out an amusing textual change introduced during the Revolution: a line from the chorus 'L'Amour triomphe', which opens the last scene, was changed from 'Sa chaîne agréable est préferable à la liberté' to 'Sa chaîne agréable est le doux charme de la volupté'; during the 1790s it was impolitic to suggest that anything was preferable to liberty!

A comparison of the scores

A table comparing the contents of *Orfeo* and *Orphée* is given below, pp. 127-34. The changes can be summarised as the adaptation of the principal role for Le Gros, the reorchestration of some numbers, and the additional material provided for Paris.

Eighteenth-century composers wrote for specific performers, but in tailoring the role of Orpheus so exactly to Le Gros' voice, Gluck was storing up trouble for the future. Le Gros had an unusually brilliant and flexible upper register, particularly from top F to B flat, while, according to his contemporaries, the notes below the G below middle C were (unsurprisingly) weak. Gluck exploited the upper range throughout the opera, so that the role lies consistently about a third higher than the conventional tenor register. He transposed the duet in Act III from G to F solely to display Le Gros' ringing top Cs; and top Ds occur in Act II to express 'L'excès de mes malheurs'. A handful of other tenors in the 1780s and 1790s seem to have attempted the role at this pitch, but when Louis Nourrit took over the part in 1809 numerous downward transpositions had to be made, and these have become the order of the day for most tenors since that time.

How important are the transpositions made for Le Gros? Critics tend automatically to deplore them, because they disturb the key sequences of the original work. There is evidence that Gluck planned the key sequences of the original *Orfeo* very carefully indeed. The three main incidents in Act I, for example, are set in three main key areas, and the relationship between the keys reflects the relationship between the incidents. The initial mourning establishes C minor as the tonic. It is followed by Orpheus's reflections on it, in the subdominant, F major: a key relationship intrinsically expressive of lowered tension. When the action moves on again, with Cupid's proposal for Eurydice's rescue, the new episode is set in the forward-moving dominant key of G major. These keys are prominent in the other acts, too (see above, pp. 41-4), and at first sight they seem crucial to Gluck's musical scheme for the opera. However, key sequences constituted the first aspect of *Orfeo* that Gluck was prepared to jettison – as early as 1769, in the transposition of the role for Millico, and again in 1774 for Le Gros. And it is idle to point out that the Paris version has an apparently even more logical structure than the Vienna score:

		Orfeo	*Orphée*
1	Mourning chorus	C minor	C minor
2	Chorus repeated (after	C minor –	C minor –
	recitative and ballet)	C major	C major
3	Orpheus's song	F major	C major

because in Gluck's earliest working of the Paris score of this act (existing in an autograph sketch) he was apparently quite happy to build a sequence of unrelated keys, destroying even the expected symmetry and continuity of the repeat of the chorus:

Orphée sketch
1 Mourning chorus in C minor
2 Repeat of chorus in D minor – D major
3 Orpheus's song in D major

So the difference between Guadagni's Orpheus and Le Gros' does not depend on the tonal structure – to Gluck it was simply not that important.

The greatest area of change between the two settings of the principal role lies in the recitative, which was almost entirely rewritten for the Paris score. In Ex. 11a and 11b we can see how the difference between the French and the Italian languages has produced a significant difference in characterisation. The Italian libretto is simpler, with short, self-contained phrases. The climax, at 'venti', is clear, but unexaggerated. By contrast, Moline's sentences are both longer and syntactically more complex. The interpolation of 'hélas' reinforces the expression of *personal* grief, and Gluck seizes on it to increase the effect of the climax, doubling the length of the high note and enriching the scoring with an extra oboe entry.

Many other examples could be quoted to show the heightened personal expression in the French score. The death of Eurydice in the Vienna score is starkly tragic. The voice and orchestra are closely bound

Ex. 11a   'This is your husband weeping, demanding to know of the gods, among the mortals seeking you, and scattering upon the winds...'

Ex. 11b 'Your weeping husband, bereaved, distracted, ceaselessly asks the whole world of nature for you. The winds, alas. . .'

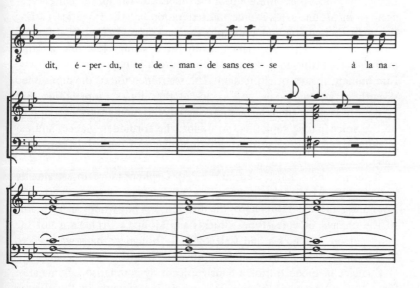

-tu -re en-tiè - re: Les vents,   hé - las!

together, and the broken vocal phrases interlock almost instrumentally
with the terse, urgent string motifs. Both the harmonies and the vocal
intervals are conventional, stylised expressions of grief (Ex. 12a). The
French score treats the same episode quite differently. Most impor-
tantly, the voices predominate over the orchestra. The longer sentences –
again – in Moline's text force the reiterations of the (identical) string
figure further apart, and thus into the background. The vocal line requires a less strictly metrical delivery; it becomes less like another
instrument slotting into the ensemble, more a purely vocal, and therefore human, means of expression. The restrained use of the diminished
seventh chord makes its appearance at the climax more telling. But
even more striking than the harmony here is the momentary overlapping
of the voice parts, depicting, no doubt, the forbidden glance, and expressing shock and surprise at the immediacy of the catastrophe (Ex.
12b).

It seems, then, that if we find the Paris Orpheus more unrestrainedly
human than his Viennese counterpart, at the same time a more tender
lover and a more dazzling hero, the difference is not wholly attributable
to the change of voice-type. Gluck's and Moline's Orpheus is not the
same person as Gluck's and Calzabigi's – though perhaps we need to
hear both scores sung by Millico to prove the point!

Changes in orchestration are insignificant by comparison. Some arise
from the replacement of the few archaic instruments in the Vienna

Ex. 12a *Orfeo:* What anguish! Oh, how my heart is torn!
      I can resist no longer. I rave, I shudder, I am mad. . .
    [He turns impetuously and looks at her]
      Ah, my treasure!
    Euridice: Great gods, what is happening?
    [Struggling to rise and falling again]
      I faint, I die.
    [Dies]
    Orfeo: Alas!

Ex. 12b   *Orphée:* Where am I? [Overcome] I cannot resist her tears.
No, the heavens do not want a greater sacrifice.
[He turns impetuously to her]
Orphée: Oh, my dear Euridice. . .
Euridice: Orphée, oh heavens!
I die. . .
[She tries to rise, and dies]
Orphée: Miserable wretch, what have I done?

score with their modern counterparts. In the opening chorus, for example, the cornetti are replaced in the Paris score by clarinets. And in Orpheus's first aria, oboes are substituted for chalumeaux and (in verse 3) clarinets for the pair of cors anglais. In 1762, Gluck was still writing for a baroque orchestra: he used the instruments available, with little thought of a standard orchestral body against which the scoring of *Orfeo* might be measured. The comparatively sparse appearance of the bassoon in the Vienna score stems from this approach. Almost certainly it doubled the cellos and basses throughout most of the opera, as part of the continuo group. The few numbers which assign it an individual stave (the Act III duet 'Vieni' and the final chorus 'Trionfi Amore' for example) are specifically those in which it does not double the continuo bass line, but reinforces the violas or (in 'Che puro ciel') holds an independent line.

The orchestra at the Académie Royale was larger and had to produce the volume of sound to fill a more spacious auditorium It is probably for this reason that – in at least some of the sources dating from the mid 1770s – the wind is used more extensively. A notable instance is the Furies' scene in Act II where, in the Vienna score, Gluck reserved the entry of the trombones to reinforce the Furies' cries of 'No!' More than one manuscript score in use in 1774 (but not the first published score) adds their sombre tone colour throughout the Furies' choruses. This is clearly part of the change from chamber opera to *tragédie lyrique:* the Paris score is grander but it lacks some of the intimate dramatic moments of the original concept.

Almost the only change in orchestration which can be regarded as an unqualified loss is the reworking of the accompaniment of 'Che puro ciel' – and this change, consisting chiefly in a simplification of texture, was made not for Paris but for Millico's performance at Parma in 1769. Gluck probably found that the orchestra at Parma did not contain a sufficiently skilful cello soloist and first flute to bring off the delicate dialogue of the original score, and having found the plainer version less demanding to rehearse, retained it for Paris. This is surely a compromise we need not retain in twentieth-century performances.

The additional numbers supplied for Paris are part of the augmentation of the chamber opera into a full-scale work. They can be identified from the table on pp. 127-34 and are discussed by their several champions in Chapter 8.

The addition which created the greatest controversy in Gluck's lifetime was undoubtedly the bravura aria which ends Act I in the Paris score, 'L'espoir renaît dans mon âme'. At this point in the enlarged

French version, Gluck clearly felt the need for a brilliant finale number, to exploit the special qualities of Le Gros' voice. (The only other Act I aria, 'Objet de mon amour', is not particularly suited to the heroic tenor.) The aria was enormously successful and Gluck had it published separately, dedicated to Le Gros, within a few months of the première of *Orphée*. It is interesting to see Gluck, so soon after penning that trenchant criticism of the 'mistaken vanity on the part of singers' and 'excessive complaisance on the part of composers' in the preface to *Alceste,* providing the very runs, high notes and cadenzas which the original *Orfeo* purported to abolish. But it was not for betraying these reform principles that Gluck was so fiercely attacked by his contemporaries. Five years after the first performances of *Orphée* – a significant time-lag, which removes much credence from the accusation – Gluck was charged with having plagiarised the aria from an opera by Ferdinando Giuseppe Bertoni. A full-scale Parisian pamphlet battle ensued, with venomous attacks from the anti-Gluck faction, detached disdain from the Gluckists, and bewildered modesty from Bertoni.

Permit me to inform you that this aria. . .has been in the hands of several amateurs in the capital for the last ten years. I have seen several copies of it in Italy, and it has been sung in various concerts, public and private. . .both before and after the first performance of *Orphée*. Gluck has had it performed before his very eyes, always ascribed to Bertoni, and *he* has not made any accusation against Bertoni – Gluck himself, who was so urgent in claiming that Jommelli had plagiarised two chords in his *Olympiade.*

(Claude-Philibert Coqueau, *Journal de Paris,* 27 July 1779)

It requires so little talent and so little merit to compose airs of the sort that closes the first act of the French *Orphée,* an air in which M. Le Gros parodies the Italian style, that M. Gluck is little tempted to rebuff the article in your journal which had the temerity to attribute it to Bertoni.

(Anon., *Journal de Paris,* 28 July 1779)

I have no wish to be drawn into a musical quarrel. . .the air was composed by me, but I do not remember in which year; I cannot even tell you if I really wrote it for *Iphigenia in Tauris* as you say I did – I rather thought it belonged to my opera *Tancred.*

(Bertoni, letter to Coqueau, 9 September 1779,
quoted in preface to Finscher's edition, 1967)

We shall never establish the truth. Perhaps a clue lies in the Gluckist's phrase 'in which M. Le Gros parodies the Italian style'. 'L'espoir renaît' is certainly a *self*-borrowing. Gluck took it from an aria he had already used twice before: the aria which opens *Il Parnasso confuso* (1765) and which appears again in the *Atto d'Aristeo,* a companion-piece to the Millico version of *Orfeo* given in Parma in 1769. But the material is too empty a parody of an Italian bravura number to stand up to claims and counter-claims of authorship. Bertoni certainly wrote a similar piece; so, no doubt, did dozens of minor Italian composers of the mid eighteenth century. Only Gluck, however, achieved permanence for his creation by incorporating it in a score of much finer and vastly more original music, where it remains as controversial as ever: dazzlingly effective when sung by the tenor voice for which it was on this occasion designed – and all too often embarrassingly unsuitable when attempted by a less flexibly voiced contralto, misled by the Viardot tradition. From the first published score of his edition of the opera (1866), we know that Berlioz' attitude to the aria was ambivalent. But he certainly seems to have sanctioned Viardot's performance, added cadenzas and all, and has thus been responsible for perpetuating an uneasy compromise. Berlioz was always determined to have his cake and eat it.

7 The opera in the nineteenth century

Berlioz and Gluck
BY EVE BARSHAM

Hector Berlioz' devotion to the operas of Gluck dates from his early years. In the library of his family home at La Côte-Saint-André, he discovered some pages of the printed score of *Orphée* which revealed to him a musical counterpart of the classical literature he had studied avidly throughout his boyhood. In his *Mémoires* (1870) he recalls that 'it was [Virgil] who found a way to my heart first of all, and widened my young imagination, by speaking to me of epic passions' (p. 9). When, in 1821, at the age of eighteen, Berlioz arrived in Paris, ostensibly to study medicine, he lost no time in his eagerness to hear Gluck's operas performed.

Circumstances were favourable: the director of the newly built Théâtre de l'Opéra, François Habeneck, was moderately progressive in his tastes, and public interest was reawakened after the lifting of Napoleon's restrictions on theatres and the reopening of the Conservatoire closed by the Bourbons. Inside the theatre, changes brought more scope to the productions. Gas lighting was installed in 1822, with the result that the auditorium could be darkened during a performance, and the stylised eighteenth-century sets had been replaced with more imaginative scenic backgrounds which could be further varied, according to the angle and the amount of light directed on them. The repertoire of this home of ultra-conservatism was also updated. Between 1821 and 1825 Berlioz was able to hear not only the major operas of Gluck, but also works by such composers as Salieri, Méhul and Spontini, works whose operatic ancestry could be traced back to Gluck. And so, as Berlioz continues in his *Mémoires:*

I read and re-read Gluck's scores. I copied them out and memorised them. I had sleepless nights because of them, and forgot about eating and drinking. I was possessed by an ecstasy, and when the anxiously awaited day came that I was at last able to hear *Iphigénie en Tauride*, I made a vow as I left the Opéra that, regardless of father, mother, uncles, aunts, grandparents and friends, I was going to be a musician.

(p. 22)

At the heart of Berlioz' fascination with Gluck's scores was the older composer's skill in 'dramatising the orchestra'. Gluck's use of the orchestra as a means of conveying the drama had been a revelation to Berlioz ever since he first heard *Iphigénie en Tauride*. Two days after his eighteenth birthday, on 13 December 1821, he wrote to his sister,

Imagine first of all an orchestra of eighty musicians who perform with such perfect ensemble that one would think it was a single instrument. The opera begins. . . The orchestra presages a storm. . . the orchestra is dully murmuring; it seems as if you heard the soughing of the wind. . . It is all in the orchestra. If you could only hear how all the situations are depicted in it.

(*Correspondance*, p. 36)

Berlioz soon discovered that the library of the Conservatoire was open to the public, and here he would spend hours copying and studying the scores. In 1882 the Italian composer Cherubini, domiciled in Paris since 1788, was made director, and it was not long before Berlioz fell foul of him, the first of their several confrontations arising from Cherubini's instigation of separate 'male' and 'female' entrance doors at the Conservatoire. Berlioz, arriving to continue his usual copying, unintentionally used the wrong door, and was eventually challenged by the director himself. The *Mémoires* record the following exchanges:

'Wh- wh- what are you doeeng 'ere?'
'As you can see, sir, I'm making a study of Gluck's scores.'
'And wh- wh- what 'ave Gluck's scores to do wiz you? 'Ow deed you get ze pairmeesion to use ze library?'
'Sir,' (I was beginning to lose my patience), 'Gluck's scores are the best examples of dramatic music that I know. . . The library is open to the public from ten till three and I am within my rights to use it'. . .
'Wh- wh- what ees your name?' he screeched, quivering with rage.
'Sir,' I replied, turning pale myself, 'my name may be well known to you one day — but you shall not have it now.'
'S- s- seize 'eem, Hottin,' he called out to the porter. . .'I'll 'ave 'eem in gaol.' So saying, to the amazement of the onlookers, the two men, master and servant, began chasing me round the tables, sending stools and desks flying in a useless attempt to catch me. Finally I escaped, and called out as I ran off laughing. . .'You won't get me or my name, and I'll be back here soon to study Gluck's scores.'

(p. 35)

This assiduous study of Gluck's work in print had made Berlioz the keenest and most critical member of the audience at the Opéra. Speaking of these very regular visits in the *Mémoires*, Berlioz describes Gluck as 'the Jove of our Olympus'. He continues:

The most ardent music-lover today can have no idea of how passionately we worshipped him. But whereas some of my friends were devotees of the faith, I can say with all due modesty that I was its high priest. If ever I noticed any lessening of their enthusiasm, I would. . .haul them off to the Opéra, often paying for their tickets myself. . .As soon as the overture began, any talking, humming, or beating time by those sitting around us was strictly taboo. . .If anyone did so, we would silence him with the famous remark devised for the occasion by a lover of music. . .'Damn these musicians, they're preventing me from hearing what this gentleman is saying.' It was equally unwise for the performers to make any alterations to the score, for I knew every note, and would sooner have died than permit the smallest tampering with the great masters to go uncontested. I did not intend waiting to protest coldly by means of the printed word at this crime against genius. No fear! I denounced the offenders on the spot, in public, and in loud, clear tones. And I can vouch for it that no other method of criticism is so efficacious. For example, one evening *Iphigénie en Tauride* was being played. I had noticed at the previous performance that cymbals had been added in the Scythians' first dance. . .which Gluck scored for strings only, and also that in Orestes' great recitative in the third act the trombones. . . had been left out. I decided that if the same mistakes occurred again, I would call attention to them. When the Scythian ballet began, I listened for the cymbals. They appeared just as they had before. Although I was boiling over with rage, I managed to control myself until the end of it, then in the following short pause I shouted at the top of my voice, 'There are no cymbals in that! Who has dared to correct Gluck?' You may imagine the consternation! The general public, who are very vague about artistic matters, and who do not care whether or not a composer's scoring is altered, failed to understand what the young lunatic down in the pit was getting so mad about. But worse was to come in the third act. The trombones in Orestes' monologue were left out as I had feared they would be, and my same voice rang out through the theatre: 'Where are the trombones? This is intolerable!'. . .At subsequent performances everything was as it should be. The cymbals were removed, and the trombones restored. I contented myself with a subdued growl of, 'Ah, that's better now.'

(pp. 49-53)

Whenever and wherever possible – and especially in print – Berlioz carried on a campaign to protect or promote Gluck's reputation as Paris became increasingly intoxicated with Italian opera in general and with Rossini in particular. In the columns of *Le Corsaire* (August 1823) he protests that 'Rossini's operas taken together can hardly bear comparison with one line of Gluck's recitative', and with irony he wonders why Rossini enthusiasts 'can hardly breathe from sheer emotion' at the pathos of his *La scala di seta* and yet are unmoved by Gluck:

because [the singers perform] so badly at the Opera, content as they are to be dramatic and sometimes even sublime. How ridiculous is Madame Branchu in the role of Clytemnestra [in *Iphigénie en Aulide*]! Why, she does not add a single note to her part, not even in the aria of Jove and his thunderbolts, though on the first verse a twelve-note roulade would admirably depict lightning and on the second, a little *martellato* would prettily stress the crushing of the Greeks. On the words 'burning ships' a chromatic scale of trills would imitate the whirling flames. Those are the things the *dilettanti* expect from singers, and as long as Madame Branchu will confine herself to making her audience shudder and weep, the *dilettanti* will say she howls.

(Quoted in Barzun, *Berlioz*, I, p. 57)

On 19 December 1825 in *Le Corsaire*, Berlioz dared to attack the powerful Castil-Blaze, critic of the *Journal des Débats*, who, denouncing Gluck's work as lacking in emotion and based on an outdated system of declamation, provoked the sarcastic rejoinder:

But who is this 'one' who no longer accepts Gluck's system?. . . who is then this implacable critic, this universal corrector of taste? He must be some great composer, a lyric poet, or at least a member of the Academy? Not at all: he is more than all these. He is M. Castil-Blaze.

(*Ibid.* p. 67)

Years later, in *Soirées de l'orchestre* (1852), the same kind of objection to Gluck as 'academic' is raised by an imaginary pupil who has come for lessons to a violinist, Adolpho D (alias Berlioz himself):

Gluck, whose scores he [Adolpho D] knew by heart (for he had copied them in order to be better acquainted with them), was his idol. He read him, played him, and sang him night and day. A misguided amateur to whom he was giving lessons in solfeggio was once incautious enough to tell him that Gluck's operas were merely shouting and plainsong. D, flushed with indignation, yanked open the drawer of his desk, took from it the ten vouchers for the fees due [to] him by this particular pupil, and flung them in his face, roaring: 'Get out of here! I don't want you or your money, and if you ever step inside this door again, I will throw you out of the window!'

(Trans. Barzun, p. 135)

In 1826, having abandoned his medical career, Berlioz officially entered the Conservatoire, though since 1823 he had already been studying composition with J.-F. Lesueur, whose enthusiasm for Gluck equalled his own. With Lesueur's encouragement he submitted a cantata, *La mort d'Orphée*, for the final stage of the Prix de Rome competition in 1827. But it was not successful; and because the pianist who played the test pieces to the adjudicators floundered over the orchestral score, it was even declared unplayable. Rediscovered only some forty years ago, the score shows how profound Gluck's influence on the young composer was: 'His study of Gluck's scores had not been in vain. What he had found in them was not simply a set of successful effects to repeat, but the principle by which timbre or orchestral color becomes an object of constant musical or expressive interest' (Barzun, *Berlioz*, I, p. 75).

In his *Grand traité d'instrumentation et d'orchestration* Berlioz goes into some detail about the orchestral effects he most admired in the score of *Orphée*. He quotes, for instance, sixteen bars of the orchestral 'growling' in Act II scene 1, where Orpheus confronts the dog monster, Cerberus, commenting that

glissandi of short notes before longer ones. . .can be extremely effective. The furious shaking of the whole orchestra by the contrabasses. . .is made more terrifying by the composer's having put it on the third inversion of the chord of the diminished seventh. . .and in order to give it all possible accentuation and vehemence he has doubled the contrabasses at the octave, not only with the violoncellos but with the violas and the entire body of violins (see Ex. [13]).

(p. 55)

Ex. 13

Later in the *Traité* Berlioz attempts to explain away an objection which certainly would not be raised by any twentieth-century listener. In the Furies' chorus in Act II of *Orphée*, F sharp and G flat are sounded simultaneously by the voices and the orchestra (see Ex. 14), and this seems to have caused some consternation to the more pedantic of Gluck's contemporaries. Berlioz explains that

Gluck has established an enharmonic relationship between two parts in an *indeterminate* key. I refer to the passage about which J. J. Rousseau and others have written so many foolish things on account of the difference which they believed existed between the G flat and the F sharp. If it were true that in performance any difference could be heard. . .this difference. . .would produce nothing but an intolerable and unmusical discord. . .Far from this, the listener is deeply stirred by a feeling of awesome grandeur which is definitely musical. It is true

Ex. 14

that he does not know precisely what the tonality is. Is it B flat? Is it G minor? He cannot tell — it does not matter much; but nothing offends him about the combination of the various instrumental and vocal parts. The F sharp of the chorus and of the first orchestra produces the marvellous effect we hear because of the unexpected way it is introduced and the feeling of wildness suggested by this vagueness of key, and not because of its supposedly acute discordance with G flat

(*Ibid.* p. 289)

Berlioz also quotes the 36-bar-long flute solo from the ballet in Act II scene 2 of the 1774 score. His accompanying comment is almost an essay in itself:

If. . .it were appropriate to give to a mournful melody a feeling not only of desolation, but also of humility and resignation, the feeble sounds of the flute in the keys of C minor and D minor especially would certainly produce the desired effect. One master only seems to have known how to make most effective use of this pale colouring; and he is Gluck. Listening to the air in D minor which he wrote for the scene of the Elysian fields in *Orphée*, one realises immediately that only a flute could play the melody. An oboe would have sounded too childlike and its tone would not have seemed sufficiently pure; the cor anglais is too grave; a clarinet would have been better, no doubt, but some of the notes would have sounded too strong, and none of the softer notes could have reduced themselves to the feeble, faint, veiled sound of the F natural of the flute medium and of the first B flat above the stave, which give so much sadness to the flute in this D minor key where those notes frequently occur. In short, neither the violin, the viola, nor the violoncello, whether alone or in combination, would adequately express this very sublime lament of a suffering, despairing spirit; it needed to be the very instrument the composer chose. And his melody is so devised that the flute lends itself to all the uneasy writhings of this eternal grief, still coloured with the passions of earthly life. It is at first a voice scarcely audible which seems to fear being overheard; then it laments softly, rising into the accent of reproach, then into that of deepest grief, the cry of a heart torn by incurable wounds, falling by degrees into complaint, regret, and the sorrowing murmur of a resigned soul. What a poet!

(Ibid. p. 153)

Despite Berlioz' total sympathy with Gluck, he was not an uncritical admirer of the older composer. He realised that Gluck had failed at times to put into practice his own reformed operatic principles, and took issue with him on the role of music in opera. In his collection of essays *À travers chants* (1862), he remarks that

When Gluck says that music in a lyric drama has no other end but to add to poetry what colour adds to drawing, I think he is guilty of a fundamental error. . .The composer's work already contains both drawing and colour; and, to carry on Gluck's simile, the words are the 'subject' of the painting, hardly anything more. . .Gluck himself, under the influence of a bad example, and being, moreover, not so great a musician as he was a composer of stage music, allowed himself to put forth that incredible inanity, the overture to *Orphée.*

(p. 150)

Berlioz' detailed knowledge of this score was to prove an incalculable influence on the future of the opera. For in middle life, shortly after he had completed his own Virgilian music drama, *Les Troyens,* he was at last given the opportunity to present Gluck's music to Paris audiences in a way calculated to redress any previous travesties or misunderstandings. He was engaged by Léon Carvalho, the most enlightened impresario of the day, to prepare a production of *Orphée* at the theatre of which Carvalho was the director, the Théâtre Lyrique. This building, of comparatively modest size, was ideal for such a presentation. The facial expressions of the actors were not lost on the audience, the words could easily be heard and the delicate instrumentation could be fully appreciated, for, as Berlioz pointed out,

It is these vast spaces. . .which seem to excuse certain composers for the insensate brutalities of their orchestration. These same vast spaces have also contributed to produce the school of singing which we now enjoy, and in which, instead of singing, it is considered right to vociferate; in which, in order to give more force to the emission of sound, the singer takes breath for every four, and often every three notes; thus breaking up and destroying every well-built phrase and every noble melody, suppressing the elisions, making frequent lines of thirteen or fourteen feet, not to mention either the splitting up of the musical rhythm, or the hiatus, or the hundred other villainies which transform melody into recitative, verse into prose and French into the dialect of Auvergne. . .[This has] brought about the howlings of tenors, basses and sopranos at the Opéra; and [has] caused the most famous singers of that theatre to merit the titles of bulls, peacocks and guinea fowls, which coarse people are accustomed to give them, as such folk do not trouble to call things otherwise than by their real names.

(*Ibid.* p. 124)

But Berlioz realised that Gluck had encountered this problem and many others during his rehearsals of *Orphée* in Paris. On one occasion, when the tenor Le Gros was, as usual, shouting out his aria 'Laissez vous toucher' ('Let my tears arouse your pity', Act II scene 1), Gluck was moved to call out, 'Monsieur! Monsieur! Be good enough to moderate your clamour. By the very devil, they don't cry out like that, even in hell!' (*ibid.*) The chorus, too, needed to be re-educated. In Gluck's time, as Berlioz recalls, they

did not act. Planted right and left upon the stage like organ pipes, they recited their lesson with desperate calm. He it was who sought to animate them; indicating every gesture and movement to be made, and so consuming himself in his efforts, that he would have succumbed to the labour had he not been gifted with so robust a nature.

(*Ibid.* p. 203)

Without the protection of Marie Antoinette, Gluck would no doubt have found his performers less co-operative. On one occasion, Vestris, the dancer, had dared to say that he could not dance to Gluck's *airs de ballet* and was commanded by the queen to apologise. Berlioz recounts that when Gluck, tall and strong, saw the dancer, who was light of build, come into the room,

he ran up to him, took him under the arms, and, singing a tune from *Iphigénie en Aulide,* danced him willy-nilly round the apartment. Afterwards, planting him breathless on a chair, he sneeringly remarked, 'Aha! You see how uncommonly good my *airs de ballet* are to dance to, since only to hear me hum one of them makes you jump about like a young goat.'

(*Ibid.* p. 125)

In preparing a revised score on which the new 1859 production would be based (a score which was eventually published in 1866), Berlioz' chief difficulty was that Gluck's original scores

were all written in happy-go-lucky style. . .In one place the composer forgets to indicate the crook of the horns, while in another he even omits the name of the wind instrument which he wishes to execute an important part. . .Sometimes he writes important notes for the bassoons on the contrabass stave and afterwards bothers no more about them, and one cannot tell what they should do next. . .Gluck says in one of his letters, 'My presence at the rehearsals of my works is as indispensable as the sun is to the creation.' I believe it. But it would have been a little less necessary if he had given himself the trouble to write with more attention; and if he had not left the executants so many intentions to guess and so many errors to rectify. . .I once saw a performance of *Iphigénie en Tauride* at Prague, which, had I not heartily laughed at it, would have made me choleric. *(Ibid.* p. 201)

Berlioz regretted Gluck's practice of indicating that the violas should play in octaves with the cellos, which could mean that they were higher than the first violins in places. He also deplored Gluck's replacement by clarinets of the two cors anglais which had been used to accompany the aria 'Piango il mio ben' ('I weep for my beloved') in Act I of the 1762 production, and took pains to reinstate them. Expression marks had sometimes been wrongly placed in both the 1764 and the 1774 engraved scores, and needed to be thoroughly revised. The contralto voices of the 1762 chorus, which had been replaced in Paris by strident *haute-contre* voices, needed to be restored, as did the part for the cornetto (for which Berlioz used a brass cornet). The cornetto was a wooden instrument with a mouthpiece of copper or brass, and its omission in Paris had left the soprano line in the opening chorus of Act I, which it should have doubled, without instrumental support. Elsewhere, in the underworld scene, trombone parts had been added in an unknown hand where Gluck had not intended them, so that his concept of trombone entries reinforcing the Furies' cries of 'Non!' was concealed and weakened. In places Moline's French text sounded inept, and needed rewriting. There were also vocal cadenzas (missing from the original, or insufficient for contemporary taste) to be supplied. Berlioz wanted to revise certain accompaniments, but he delegated this task to Saint-Saëns, remarking that he himself could hardly be expected to rescore the work of Gluck, when he had spent his life persecuting others for doing just that!

During the autumn of 1859, Berlioz had also to teach the cast how to sing their parts, act, dress and dance. He discovered that, understandably, the dancers had only very hazy notions as to how ancient Greek shades in Hades deported themselves. Carvalho, despite his amiability, found it hard to accept that Berlioz wanted to present either *Orphée* or nothing at all — 'without Castilblazade of any kind'. The impresario's suggestion that the score should be supplemented with music from other Gluck operas merely provoked Berlioz to remark upon his manifold good intentions and that his hell should be paved with them. But by now, as Barzun describes, Berlioz was a seasoned commander-in-chief. He could make up programs, cope with officialdom, draft publicity notices, watch the accounting, see that notables were sent tickets, and kindle the zeal of janitors; he could rehearse, conduct, train the amateurs, cajole the professionals, disarm the grumblers, and impart passion to the mass. He knew how to word reminders and sugarcoat admonitions; he could induce the press to write, the printers to print, and the public to come.

(*Berlioz*, I, p. 481)

In *À travers chants*, Berlioz himself admits that 'Despotism is necessary; supremely intelligent in kind no doubt, but all the same – despotism. It must be military despotism, the despotism of a commander-in-chief or of an admiral in time of war' (p. 215).

The production of *Orphée*, to which all the gruelling preparations were leading, was to be a 'stroke of audacity', a crossing of the Italian and the French versions of the score. Crucial to this new hybrid was Berlioz' choice of a contralto voice, to readopt the original vocal register of the Italian Orfeo. The distinguished creator of the role was to be Pauline Viardot-Garcia, a member of the renowned Spanish musical family. Her father, the tenor Manuel Garcia, was also a composer of operas, and certainly the most illustrious singing teacher in Europe during the mid nineteenth century. Her sister, Marie Malibran, enjoyed an equally wide reputation as a singer, but Viardot might well be claimed as one of the most influential women in the history of music. Her vocal compass was exceptionally wide, extending over three octaves, and apart from her talents as a singer she had literary and artistic ability, and spoke several languages. As a pianist and composer she was well known for her adaptations for voice of such instrumental pieces as Chopin's mazurkas. Since her teens she had included arias by Gluck in her repertoire, and significantly it was only after she had agreed to sing the part of Orpheus that the rest of the preparations for the production were set in motion. Berlioz describes how her performances united an 'imperious verve with a profound sensibility. . .Her gesture is well moderated, being both noble and true to nature, and the expression of her face, always powerful, is even more so in the dumb scenes than in those in which it merely aids the accentuation of the song' (*ibid.* p. 116).

The table of numbers (below, pp. 127-34) gives an idea of the changed order of some of the vocal and orchestral numbers, and of the transpositions involved in the reversion to the contralto range for Orpheus's part. This change of register is much more than just a technicality: if the original male castrato tone gave the character of Orpheus an 'extra-human', mythical quality, which had been replaced by the humanity of the tenor voice in the 1774 version, something near to the original vocal register could be restored and also the 'human' quality retained by the use of a female voice. In general, Berlioz followed the score of the 1774 version, with a few modifications of tempo and time signature, reverting to the Italian score only where he felt there was some musical or dramatic advantage. Thus though the recitatives in general follow the French version, the final recitative in Act I reverts to the Italian version, and Berlioz felt it might even prove a fitting conclusion to the act, if rounded off with a twelve-bar orchestral passage (which is printed as an appendix at the end of his score). In this way, the out-of-character bravura aria which he believed (mistakenly) to be the work of Gluck's contemporary Bertoni might be dispensed with

4a   Pauline Viardot-Garcia as Orpheus

Mme. Viardot-Garcia's cadence in Gluck's aria "L'espoir renait"

4b   Pauline Viardot-Garcia's cadenza to 'L'espoir renaît dans mon
      âme'

altogether. This notorious aria appears in G major (transposed from the original key of B flat) in the score of Berlioz' production with a remark in the publisher's preface to the effect that since Gluck, however surprisingly, included the aria in his printed score, 'we do not think we have the right to leave it out'. It had been rescored, and Viardot had made some alterations to the vocal part, and supplied a cadenza. The evidence, therefore, is strong that Berlioz used this aria in his performances of the opera, despite his reservations.

Thirteen months before the first performance of Berlioz' revised *Orphée,* the Orpheus parody to end all parodies, Offenbach's *Orphée aux enfers,* had opened at the Bouffes-Parisiens theatre, creating a huge *succès de scandale.* It proved to be a landmark in the history of comic opera. Accused of blaspheming antiquity, Offenbach had used the myth as a vehicle for satirising the government and social conditions (incidentally also making fun of Gluck's Orpheus's lament, as all previous parodies had done). It was in this unpromising atmosphere of satire and disrespect that Berlioz' own production opened, on 19 November 1859, and no more vivid description of the spectacular première can be found than the letter written two days later by Viardot herself to the composer and conductor Julius Rietz:

I shall play. . .three times a week till the public and I can stand it no longer. My costume. . .[is] a white tunic falling to the knees – [and]

a white mantle caught up at both shoulders in the manner of Apollo. Flowing tresses, curled, with the crown of laurel. A chain of gold to support the sword, whose sheath is red. A red cord around the waist — buskins white, laced with red. . .Well, people embraced each other in the passage-ways during the intermissions, they wept, they laughed for delight, they trampled the floor — in a word, there was a turmoil, a jubilation such as I have never seen in Paris. . .

I fancy you haven't an idea of the effect which can be produced by the stage-setting of the scene in the Elysian Fields. . .The chorus ['Viens dans ce séjour'] is sung in the wings, Orphée remaining quite alone on the stage. Then, during the delicious instrumental number, the Shades come on in small, curious groups. Orphée seeks for Euridice among them — by the end of the number the entire chorus is on the stage. This scene in pantomime received two rounds of applause. . .The Duo with Euridice [Marie Sax] (a lovely, untrained voice) also made a great impression, but the number which marked the culminating point was the air 'J'ai perdu mon Euridice'. I think I have discovered three good ways of delivering the *motif*. The first time, sorrowful amazement, almost motionless. The second, choked with tears (the applause lasted two minutes, and they wanted an encore!!!), the third time, outbursts of despair. My poor Euridice remarked, as she arose: 'Mph! I thought that would last forever!'

('Letters to Julius Rietz', pp. 44-6)

Berlioz' own account of the same performance is not without some critical observations, but his praise for Viardot is tempered only by criticism of her unjustified pausing on top G towards the end of Orpheus's lament in Act III, adding roulades to one of the recitatives and altering certain words. He agrees that the culminating triumph of her part was the aria 'J'ai perdu mon Euridice'. Remembering Gluck's warning, 'change the slightest shade of movement or of accent in that air and you make a puppet dance of it', he deplores those ignorant admirers who applauded before the end, remarking contemptuously that 'some persons would call out "encore" during "To be or not to be" in *Hamlet'* (*À travers chants,* p. 120).

The overwhelming success of the new *Orphée* — it ran for 150 performances — brought fame and fortune to Carvalho as well as considerable royalties to Berlioz. It had been a source of satisfaction to him that not only had such distinguished members of the audience as Flaubert and Dickens been impressed with it (Dickens is said to have been moved to tears), but also that the random public composed (in Viardot's words) of 'musicians, amateurs, pedants, bald heads, the world of boredom, youthful lions, etc.' ('Letters to Julius Rietz', p. 46) had reacted favourably. None the less he suspected that a new kind of audience hypocrisy might arise:

Orphée begins to have a vogue which is rather disquieting. We hope Gluck is not going to be fashionable. . . Ought the entire Polonius class [i.e. those who are not genuine opera lovers] feel obliged to stay awake. . . when they'd rather go to their favourite parodies in a theatre which it is forbidden to name? Why shouldn't they say, 'What a bore!'. . . (I do not quote the exact expression in use by Messrs Polonius as it is not quite recognised in literature). . . 'We are going to see Punch and Judy in the Champs-Elysées for consolation. We consider that we have been robbed!'

(*À travers chants*, p. 122)

Performances of the new *Orphée* took place in London (at Covent Garden) in 1860 and elsewhere in Europe in the following decade. *Alceste* was also revised and produced in Paris in 1861 and subsequently. Now suffering from deteriorating health (he died in 1869), Berlioz was too unwell to undertake the preparation of the printed score of the new *Orphée*, which was published by Heinze of Leipzig in 1866, but he made corrections to the proofs and was able to correspond with the editor, Alfred Dörfell. This compromise between the French and the Italian versions of the opera was certainly not to prove the final or only possible solution of the need to reconcile the two – almost every subsequent production has necessitated further modifications – but the 1859 version provided a new starting-point, making possible a new valuation not only of Gluck's work but of the wider field of eighteenth-century opera before Mozart, and thus providing a further example of an Orpheus production which has made operatic history. Well might Berlioz, in 1856, say half-seriously to his sister: 'It seems to me that if Gluck were to come back to life he would say of me, "This is without doubt my son." I'm not modest, am I?' (quoted in *Hector Berlioz*, Bibliothèque Nationale (Paris, 1969), p. 31).

After Berlioz
BY PATRICIA HOWARD

Berlioz' reworking of Gluck's opera brought about a new enthusiasm for the work across Europe and in the Americas. Not that Berlioz' edition became in any sense the standard version; there was no standard version. Throughout the nineteenth century, the title role was sung nearly as often by a tenor as by a contralto. Translations of the libretto into the local language – for example Czech, Dutch, Flemish, Norwegian, Catalan, Finnish – abounded, and at the same time, back-translations were made into Italian which became increasingly distant from Calzabigi's. Gluck himself having established a precedent to adapt and modify the opera, new versions were constantly being tried out. Liszt, for example, wrote a new prelude and closing music for the performance he directed at Weimar on 16 February 1854, the prelude later becoming an independent symphonic poem, *Orpheus*. Even the pastiche given in London in 1792 (see above, p. 65) was revived in New York on 25 May 1863. In London, the prevailing tone colours of Berlioz' contralto version coincided with the strong oratorio tradition and the work was revived regularly in this version, taking on an almost religious aura as a long line of plummy contraltos made the title role their own.

With the twentieth century came the first stirrings of the movement towards authenticity. In 1914 the original score of the 1762 version was printed in the Denkmäler der Tonkunst in Österreich series, and a performance of this was given at Lauchstedt on 19 June 1914. It must be mentioned, however, that the work was sung in German and the role of Orpheus was given to a baritone. Nevertheless, the long climb back to the rediscovery of what Gluck actually wrote had begun. That this rediscovery is still in the making will become apparent in the next chapter.

8 The opera in the twentieth century

The situation in the twentieth century is obviously and perhaps inevitably confused. Three major versions of the opera are available, and as many compromises between them as there are publishers and conductors who have chosen to present the opera to the public. To avoid giving my own prejudices a more permanent and influential status than they merit, I have invited three distinguished musicians to defend the version each has personally championed, to justify the practicability of his choice, and to demonstrate its musical and dramatic superiority over the alternatives. Each was asked to make his defence as eloquent as possible, so there are some direct contradictions between accounts, and some overlapping with material found elsewhere in the book.

Berlioz: the best of both worlds
BY SIR CHARLES MACKERRAS

Although Gluck composed *Orfeo* twice, first in Italian in 1762 for the castrato contralto Guadagni, and again in French in 1774 for the tenor Le Gros, it has hardly ever been performed using exclusively one version or the other, and in fact neither of these original versions is wholly practicable for performance in our own time.

The original Italian version of *Orfeo* was performed by both contralto and soprano castrato singers throughout the second half of the eighteenth century. We cannot, however, perform this original version of the opera today. It is no solution to substitute a counter-tenor for the castrato voice, since the differences in timbre and volume are considerable.

Twelve years after *Orfeo* had first seen the light of day, Gluck was invited to make a French version for the Opéra in Paris. In this, the main role of Orpheus was rearranged for a tenor. Gluck in fact rewrote the whole role, often transposing the keys of the arias and entirely recomposing the recitative sections. Since the orchestra and chorus at the Opéra were exceptionally large, and the *mise-en-scène* particularly luxurious, the work now took on an entirely different character. From a short, pastoral opera, it became transformed into a full-blown *tragédie-opéra*. Although Le Gros was acclaimed by the Paris public for his performance of the title role, the part was adapted almost too precisely to his unusual voice: the Paris score lies impossibly high for a normal tenor, going up at times to high D, and so, like the castrato version, this reworking of the opera is virtually unperformable nowadays.

Despite the improvements made to the work for Paris, many people felt that Gluck's original conception of Orpheus as a male contralto was more suited to the musical and dramatic intensity of the opera. In 1859, Berlioz, that great admirer of Gluck, made a version of the opera for the famous young mezzo-soprano Pauline Viardot-Garcia. He did not, however, return to the original contralto version, but rearranged and retransposed the Paris version into keys more suitable for a mezzo. The opera in this new form was, of course, still in French, but soon Berlioz' version was translated into other languages, and became re-translated back into Italian. Of the many Italian retranslations of the Paris version, two are still performed today. The translation published by Ricordi is somewhat nearer to Calzabigi's original Italian than that published by Novello in England and Peters in Germany, but all of these editions use Berlioz' version, and it is this which is normally performed today. Its tessitura is much more comfortable for a mezzo-soprano, the original Italian version being awkwardly low. In recent years, however, attempts have been made to reinstate the original Italian version, partly to suit singers with exceptionally good low notes, but also because today's taste prefers a work as the composer wrote it, rather than 'tampered with', even when the 'tamperer' is a Berlioz. Admirable as this ideal is, performing the Italian version exactly as Gluck wrote it in 1762 means omitting some of the most famous and beautiful passages in the work, notably the dance of the Blessed Spirits, the Furies' dance, Eurydice's aria and the trio. For Paris Gluck also extended two of Orpheus's most famous arias, 'Che farò' and 'Deh! placatevi', so that a return to the original constitutes a weakening. Apart from anything else, the Italian version unadulterated by anything from Paris would not fill an evening at the opera. It is sometimes given with Gluck's ballet *Don Juan* – an interesting pairing, since the ballet contains the Furies' dance that Gluck added to the Paris score (see above, p. 46). Double bills, however (apart from *Cav.* and *Pag.*), are notoriously bad box office.

The question as to whether the female voice – mezzo or contralto –

can come sufficiently near to that of an eighteenth-century castrato to be an acceptable substitute is open to dispute. Berlioz, who might well have heard castrati, decided in favour. The strongest evidence in support of his opinion comes from what is known of performance practice in early-eighteenth-century opera, when an entire cast often consisted of soprano register voices and the roles were divided between castrato and female voices almost at random. Even as late as Rossini, this equivalence was widely understood: in his early comic opera *L'equivoco stravagante,* the hero protects his mistress from the attentions of an elderly admirer by telling him that she is a castrato in disguise! Be this as it may, however, Gluck's known readiness to alter Orpheus from a castrato contralto role to a soprano (in 1769) and then to a tenor (in 1774) shows that he was less interested in a specific voice-type than in the ability and personality of the singer.

There is thus a dilemma for any opera house that plans a revival of *Orfeo;* the original Italian version is too short, sometimes too primitive, and often too low for the mezzo-soprano voice; the Paris version, though a great improvement in most respects, is so high that few tenors can cope with it. Apart from the vocal difficulty, the essential atmosphere of noble tragedy is impaired by the high-lying tessitura, and one instinctively feels that the contralto or mezzo voice is more suitable to the character of the music. Various attempts have been made to get the best of both worlds and to use a mixture of the two versions. This was done, for example, at Covent Garden in 1969 when Sir George Solti conducted the new production of *Orfeo* in a version prepared by myself. It was based on the Italian version with additions from the French. For my version at Covent Garden in 1972, I decided to approach it the other way round. Believing that neither authentic version is theatrically viable, I based my score on Berlioz' version in an Italian translation. This had the dual advantage of suiting Shirley Verrett's voice (though she has sung both versions in her time) and containing all the most famous pieces in their most developed (and most familiar) form. When I came to do the opera in the same year at the Metropolitan, New York, Marilyn Horne accepted the same version almost without change.

Let us analyse the differences between the two versions, not forgetting that the French version has been transposed for mezzo-soprano by Berlioz and translated into Italian. Only the arias, ensembles and ballets will be commented on, the recitatives being almost entirely different in both versions. Though the recitatives deal with identical emotions and situations, as a general rule those of the Italian version keep low in the voice and the melodies have a recurring downward tendency, whereas the French recitatives are on the high side and tend to be rising melodies.

The overture is identical in both versions, and the opening chorus and pantomime nearly so. 'Chiamo il mio ben così' is rescored, extending the echo effects, and the part of Cupid is extended and varied. In Vienna he had one long aria, in which he describes how Orpheus must not look at Eurydice. In Paris, this aria was cut in half, omitting the awkwardly low-lying first verse, and a charming aria introducing the character was placed before it.

Following Cupid's exit, Gluck raided his opera *Il Parnasso confuso* for a bravura aria to bring the first act to a proper close. Originally a short piece of orchestral music had represented Orpheus's descent into Hades, and it is even possible that this scene followed without a break in the simpler framework of the first Vienna performance. (In the version given in 1769 in Parma, with the soprano Millico singing Orpheus, the whole opera was given without a break, being the last act of an evening's varied entertainment called *Le feste d'Apollo*.) The bravura aria 'Addio, miei sospiri' ('L'espoir renaît dans mon âme') is certainly out of keeping with the lofty character of the rest of the opera, and Gluck was even accused of stealing it from another composer. However, an aria at the end of the first act is more suitable than a short recitative or a few bars of orchestral music, particularly if there is to be a long interval between the acts for an effective change of scene.

In the Hades scene, Gluck added for Paris a bravura ending to the aria 'Deh! placatevi' and inserted the Furies' dance (taken from his ballet *Don Juan* referred to above). Strangely enough, this Furies' dance has thematic links with the choruses in Hades, although it was written a year before the Vienna *Orfeo*. Any other differences between the versions in this scene are insignificant.

On the other hand, the scene in Elysium has the most far-reaching differences. Apart from the addition of an *air de ballet*, taken from *Paride ed Elena*, Gluck composed two new pieces for Paris, the flute solo in the dance of the Blessed Spirits and an air with chorus for Eurydice. Of these, the former has become Gluck's most familiar piece. Its gorgeous, haunting melody seems to sum up his whole musical character, and one can hardly imagine *Orfeo* without it. Eurydice's aria, too, is one of the loveliest pieces in the opera and serves to introduce her earlier than had originally been the case. In some scores this aria is assigned to 'A Blessed Spirit', possibly because it was thought inappropriate for Eurydice to express such happy sentiments on her departure from the world! There is, however, no justification for this change and it is clear that Gluck intended the air for Eurydice.

Most of the Paris alterations consist of an extension or a development of Gluck's first ideas. The second version of Orpheus's arioso 'Che
puro ciel', however, is a simplification of the original. Not only is the
interweaving obbligato of flute and cello cut out, but the number is
considerably shortened. The chorus interjection 'Giunge Euridice' is
also cut, and we proceed to the chorus 'Vieni a' regni'. Gluck extended
this and its repeat, 'Torna, o bella', for Paris, and during rehearsals he
added an orchestral epilogue to bring the act to a close.

In Act III, the new recitatives for Paris are much tighter and more
dramatic. The opening duet is virtually the same except that Gluck
made use of the clarinets available in Paris instead of the original oboes.
In Eurydice's aria 'Che fiero momento' Gluck added a part for Orpheus
in the middle slow section, thus changing it from an aria into a dramatic
duet.

From here on, the Paris version increases in dramatic tension, the
death of Eurydice being particularly poignant with the two voices unit-
ing for one last note. Orpheus's desperate recitative before the great aria
'Che farò' reaches a much tenser and more tragic climax than in the
Viennese original, and in the aria itself Gluck added a despairing rising
coda which heightens the atmosphere of noble tragedy, not only of the
aria itself, but of the whole scene; compare Ex. 15a, the Paris coda,
with Ex. 15b, the resigned 'dying fall' of the Italian ending. A further

Ex. 15a

Ex. 15b

point to notice in the aria is that the phrase 'Che farò senza il mio ben'
appears in the Italian version as even notes (Ex. 16a), but in the French

che   fa   -   rò   sen   -   za   il   mio   ben?

Ex. 16a

Rien   n'é   -   ga   -   le   mon   a   -   mour

Ex. 16b

score the violin parts are dotted, implying that the vocal line would have been dotted too (Ex. 16b). The reason for this change is not clear, unless it was the written record of a variant usually sung, perhaps showing the influence of the French tendency to use *notes inégales* even as late as 1774 and even in disjunct movement.

In the final scenes of reunion and festive ballet the Vienna version simply had recitative, followed by five dances and the final vaudeville for the three principals and chorus. In Paris the custom was to have a ballet after the end of the singing, the whole thing being rounded off by a lengthy chaconne. Gluck therefore rearranged the scenes as follows. After the recitative in which Cupid resuscitates Eurydice, there is a trio of rejoicing, 'Gaudio, gaudio' or 'Divo Amore', depending on which Italian translation is used. Gluck 'lifted' this from *Paride ed Elena*. After the trio comes the vaudeville finale, 'Trionfi Amore' (slightly extended to accommodate the higher key for the tenor), followed by seven ballet numbers, some of them taken from the original version and redistributed, and some, including the magnificent final chaconne, raided from earlier operas. Nowadays the complete ballet is rarely if ever done, as the old Parisian tradition of a *ballet-divertissement* to end an opera has disappeared. The first edition of the Paris version prints the trio in the middle of the ballet, after the vocal finale. This is probably a printer's error because the libretto gives the trio, logically, before the vaudeville, and a report of the première in the *Journal des Beaux-Arts* describes the trio as being sung immediately after Eurydice is brought back to life.

To sum up, not to use the Paris version would be to lose some of the best-loved and most theatrically effective music Gluck ever composed. But to forego the contralto register for the expression of Orpheus's grief would be an almost equal deprivation. Gluck wrote his two

Orpheus operas in such a way that we are forced to arrive at a compromise, and we are fortunate that so great a musical dramatist as Berlioz pointed the way.

[Perhaps it is not too frivolous to suggest that the *notes inégales* (see above) occurred to Gluck because of the text at this point, 'Rien n'égale mon malheur' ('amour' in Berlioz' edition)? – P.H.]

Orphée et Euridice: Gluck's final solution
BY TOM HAMMOND

Christoph Willibald Gluck bequeathed no less than three versions of his opera to posterity, and he has been followed by a procession of composers and others who have left a further bewildering series of arrangements of the score, to the confusion of the musical world in general. It should be noted that Gluck's three versions of *Orfeo* were all specifically written, in accordance with the prevailing custom, for a male protagonist, and there was no question of the role's being assumed by a female singer in the composer's lifetime.

By 1774, Gluck had already composed some fifty works for the stage in a variety of styles ranging from operas, *feste teatrali* and vaudevilles to *opéras comiques* and ballets, so that by the time he arrived in Paris under the protection of his erstwhile pupil Marie Antoinette, to write what were to prove his final and greatest masterpieces, he was an immensely experienced operatic composer who had, moreover, something very new to say. In view of this, it is surely reasonable to defend the much-maligned Paris revision and to suggest that Gluck's own final thoughts about his *Orphée* at least deserve respectful and serious consideration as the definitive version of his *chef-d'œuvre*.

The sound of the French *haute-contre* (a natural high-lying tenor voice) was obviously something quite different from that of the modern English counter-tenor, for example, whose gentler and more ecclesiastical falsetto would be ineffective, if not inaudible, in a dramatic role in a large theatre. The use of the *haute-contre* persisted in the French operas of Rossini and native composers until the arrival of the *tenore baritonale* towards the middle of the last century. By then it was no longer regarded as a contestant for serious romantic roles and was relegated to comic or character parts, for which it is in fact still used by twentieth-century composers, such as Shostakovich and Janáček.

It is clear that the *haute-contre*, at his best, possessed a vocal strength and brilliance of execution, allied to an altogether exceptional upward extension of compass, which is rare today. The music for this voice is printed in Gluck's orchestral score in the alto clef, and it might be noted that the female contralto, although common elsewhere, seems to have been non-existent in France, as it was not even employed in the opera chorus. When Gluck revised his *Orfeo* for Paris, he was compelled to use the noisy *haute-contre* in his splendid choruses, sometimes to great effect, as in the opening scene of Act II of *Orphée.*

The following quotation, from an account by Romain Rolland, will give some further idea of the extraordinary conditions at the Paris Académie Royale in 1774, when Gluck arrived on the scene:

Dramatic effect is, first and last, the main object of Gluck's music. . . It goes without saying that with such ideas Gluck could scarcely help being led to that reform of the orchestra and operatic singing which people of taste were so earnestly desiring. After his arrival in Paris it was the first thing that claimed his attention. He attacked the unspeakable chorus, which sang in masks, without any gestures – the men being ranged on one side with their arms crossed, and the women on the other with fans in their hands. He attacked the still more unspeakable orchestra, who played in gloves so as not to dirty their hands, or to keep them warm; and who spent their time noisily tuning up and in wandering about and talking, just as they pleased. But the most difficult people to deal with were the singers, who were vain and very unruly. Rousseau. . .says: 'The Opera is no longer what it used to be – a company of people paid to perform in public. It is true that they are still paid, and that they perform in public; but they have become a Royal Academy of Music, a kind of royal court, and a law unto themselves, with no particular pride in either truth or equity.' Gluck mercilessly obliged his 'academicians' to rehearse for six months at a time, excusing no faults, and threatening to fetch the queen, or to return to Vienna, every time there was any rebellion. It was an unheard-of thing for a composer to get obedience from operatic musicians. People came running to these bellicose rehearsals as if they were plays. . .

He curtailed the dancing, so far as possible, and only allowed it to form an integral part of the action, as may be seen in the ballet of the Furies, or that of the spirits of the blest in *Orphée*. With Gluck the ballet, therefore, lost some of the delightful exuberance it had had in Rameau's operas; but what it lost in originality and richness it gained in simplicity and purity; and the dance airs in *Orphée* are like classic bas-reliefs, the frieze of a Greek temple.

(*Musiciens d'autrefois*, trans. Blaiklock, pp. 296-9)

And Rolland concludes: 'All through Gluck's operas we find this simplicity and clearness, the subordination of the details of a work to the unity of the whole, and an art that was great and popular and intelligible – the art dreamed of by the Encyclopaedists' (*ibid.* p. 299).

Gluck revised his *Orfeo* to a new French text by Pierre-Louis Moline (based on Calzabigi's Italian libretto, with additions) for the presentation of the work in Paris in August 1774, a few months after the success of *Iphigénie en Aulide*. Much of the Italian score was carried over, but the composer added some new pieces for Paris and also provided new recitatives to accommodate both the French text and the particular vocal requirements of the *haute-contre* protagonist. Quite apart from the vexed question of the adaptations and transpositions to which Gluck was obliged to resort for Le Gros, the French score has many felicities and much new grandeur, which confirm it to be superior, musically and dramatically, to the original and more modest Vienna version.

Gluck's new *tragédie-opéra*, entirely on its own merits, enjoyed an enormous and lasting popular success in Paris, where the public was, of course, quite unacquainted with the earlier Italian version. Writers of the day have recorded the astonishing effect which this opera had on French audiences. The following extract from the correspondence of a certain Mlle de Lespinasse is a case in point:

The impression that the music of *Orphée* made upon me was so profound, so touching so disturbing, so overwhelming, that I found it impossible to describe my feelings. I experienced such sadness, happiness and emotion. . .I go to hear *Orphée* frequently and I go alone. . .this music drives me mad and my soul longs avidly for all this sorrow.

(Quoted in *Orphée et Euridice*, ed. F.A. Gevert
(Paris 1901), introduction)

And Jean-Jacques Rousseau writes that, 'as it is possible to discover so much pleasure in the space of two hours, I concede that life is still good for something' (*ibid.*).

Orphée remained in the repertoire of the Opéra for more than fifty years, but after the last main revival in 1830 Gluck's operas were temporarily supplanted in the public's favour by the new grand operatic spectacles of Meyerbeer. However, in 1859, *Orphée* was again successfully revived, this time at the Théâtre Lyrique, in a new and controversial arrangement by Berlioz for the great operatic star Pauline Viardot-Garcia, at the time when the cult of the *travestie* was at its height and the romantic character of the female contralto was being rediscovered. Berlioz' brilliant adaptation has the glory of having rescued the opera from possible oblivion; the disappearance of the artificial castrato and the natural-voiced *haute-contre* rendered Gluck's scores, as he conceived them, virtually unsingable by other voices. By adapting the role of Orpheus for a female singer, however, Berlioz has succeeded in permanently preserving the opera in a false dramatic light — so much so, that most opera-goers now expect to hear a contralto in the title role, being unaware that any more authentic version exists.

The passage of time has left the world with an enchanted view of the legendary Orpheus in the shape of a romantic, youthful figure with a supreme talent for matters musical and one whose voice had the power to melt the hardest of hearts. But this is really only part of the story, for Orpheus was also a notable warrior, one of the band of Argonauts who accompanied Jason in his search for the golden fleece. This warlike side of his character is not much stressed in the opera, but the existing overture and the trumpets added by Gluck to his 1774 score might be considered as a martial echo, whilst the interpolated bravura aria at the end of the revised first act could be thought of dramatically as a species of battle-cry, when the hero voices his defiance of the dread powers of the underworld, as he dons his armour and girds on his sword, amidst showers of coloratura, and prepares to rescue his lost bride. Furthermore, the victorious Orpheus is finally transported by Cupid to the Temple of Love in Elysium, where he is greeted by a jubilant host of heroes and heroines — a pre-Wagnerian Valhalla, as it were, which is surely no place for a female warrior-hero *en travestie*. Is it possible for such a singer, however great an actress, however luscious of voice or noble of bearing, to portray a bereaved warrior-husband with anything approaching dramatic conviction, especially in scenes with two other female singers, one of whom, to complicate matters still further, is also *en travestie?* Under these conditions the opera becomes little more than a ravishing concert in costume, where suspension of disbelief has to work overtime, in direct opposition to Gluck's and Calzabigi's avowed intentions as expounded in the famous preface to *Alceste*.

In Britain particularly, where there has been such a strong and splendid tradition of religious oratorio, Orpheus has for far too long been the province of the deep, maternal contralto, of a particularly English and quite untheatrical quality, causing the opera to lose practically all dramatic verisimilitude in the theatre. The substitution of a female contralto for the original artificial alto is not really a recreation of the actual sound involved, as a woman's voice inevitably deploys entirely extraneous and disturbing sexual overtones, which are not only inappropriate to the personality of Orpheus, but also do very little to conjure up the elegiac and other-worldly character of the castrato voice as history describes it.

Though we must reluctantly concede that the 1762 version is now unsingable for want of a castrato, the case for the 1774 version is by no means so dire. A modern tenor who can sing Rossini's *Count Ory,* Donizetti's *Lucia* or Bellini's *Puritani* would very likely be able to encompass Gluck's Orpheus, if certain of the most trying passages were discreetly transposed down a tone where necessary, thus to return, incidentally, to the actual pitch of Gluck's and Berlioz' day. *Orfeo* would then only need to be approached in the spirit of passionate and noble opera-tragedy, instead of sanctimonious opera-oratorio which has for long cast a gloomy shadow over so many performances in Britain and elsewhere.

Numerous revivals based on Berlioz' adaptation have been given in Britain during the present century, with a notable procession of distinguished ladies, from Louise Kirkby Lunn, Clara Butt and Mary Jarred to Kathleen Ferrier, Yvonne Minton, Shirley Verrett and Janet Baker, as protagonist. Revivals of the 1774 version, however, have been few and far between, chiefly owing to the difficulty of casting the leading role. The first attempt seems to have been that given in French in conjunction with the Colonel de Basil Ballet Company at the Royal Opera House, Covent Garden, during the Beecham season of 1937, with the tenor André Burdino. In 1965 the Misses Radford produced the opera in Falmouth with the Welsh tenor David Parker, using an edition based on the adaptation by Henri Vidal for the Opéra Comique (Paris, 1921). In 1967 Sadler's Wells Opera mounted a full-scale presentation at Rosebery Avenue in English (omitting some of the ballet music), with Alexander Young in the title role. In 1972 *Orphée* was given at Harlow, Essex, in a small-scale production, using Finscher's edition of 1967 for tenor, the role being sung by Jeffrey Talbot in the original tessitura and at modern pitch, which is now almost a tone higher than in Gluck's day. The same singer also appeared in a somewhat controversial London production in 1971, when the Vidal adaptation was again pressed into service. Since these two performances in the early 1970s, Gluck's version of 1774 seems to have gone unheard in Britain.

A note on the aria di bravura 'L'espoir renaît dans mon âme'
BY TOM HAMMOND

The authorship of the aria for the protagonist which concludes Act I of the 1774 Paris *Orphée et Euridice* eventually became a matter of doubt, and it was at one time generally attributed to Ferdinando Bertoni (1725-1813), a contemporary of Gluck and a minor but industrious Italian composer who was rash enough to write another *Orfeo* in 1776, on Calzabigi's text. In certain nineteenth-century editions of Gluck's opera in which 'Addio, miei sospiri' (or 'L'espoir renaît', or 'Amour, viens rendre', as it was variously known in French) was printed, it was clearly attributed to Bertoni, though the opera from which it was said to be taken was not always the same.

From the evidence available, it is now quite certain that the music is by Gluck, and it is probable that in its earliest version it was sung by the castrato Guadagni (the first Orpheus) at the coronation of the Emperor Joseph II at Frankfurt-am-Main in 1764, though this performance is now disputed. Gluck made further use of it in his *Il Parnasso confuso,* given at Schönbrunn the following year for the marriage of the same emperor, and it appears once more in his *Aristeo,* a work which formed part of another court entertainment for another royal marriage, at Parma in 1769.

It seems that the piece, with new words, was imitated by Bertoni in his opera *Tancredi,* given at Turin in 1767, with such success that when Gluck once more made use of his own aria, presumably at the last minute for the Paris version of *Orphée,* he was ironically accused of having imitated Bertoni! From this arose the legend that the aria was by the latter composer, a legend that took root and flourished until musical scholarship eventually unearthed the true facts.

It is related that at the time of the first production of the French *Orphée,* the *haute-contre* Le Gros requested Gluck to provide him with an aria to enable him to conclude the first act with maximum effect (his predecessor, Guadagni, had been less demanding in Vienna in 1762). Gluck, somewhat surprisingly, allowed him to sing an adaptation of this old-style composition (typical of his writing for the bravura castrato), and although it had already been used on three previous occasions, it was finally incorporated into the full score of *Orphée,* in the key of B flat, in 1774. What is perhaps still more surprising is that Berlioz himself should have allowed the piece to be performed in his own 1859 arrangement of Gluck's opera (this time in G major), and we may presume that it was retained at the request of yet another singer, namely Pauline Viardot-Garcia, who wanted it for the same reason as her predecessor Le Gros.

As originally written by Gluck, this *cheval-de-bataille* was already encrusted with conventional roulades and syncopations, calling for some considerable virtuosity on the part of the performer, but Viardot, aided and abetted by Saint-Saëns, went very much further. Quite possibly under the impression that the aria was not by Gluck anyway and was therefore not sacrosanct, Saint-Saëns rescored the accompaniment for a large orchestra, while the vocal hazards were magnified exceedingly by the addition of new, dazzling and extravagant divisions, ranging over a compass of two and a half octaves and culminating in an astounding final cadenza (the moment for which had been conventionally provided by Gluck). The aria thus became a veritable show-stopper in the hands of a great vocal virtuoso in the Garcia family tradition, who was also no mean dramatic actress. No wonder that all Paris flocked to see the new *Orphée* with such an exciting protagonist. In his *À travers chants* Berlioz somewhat drily reproves Viardot for an excess of elaboration (see above, p. 96) – but it was an excess which even he, it seems, was powerless to control.

Although this piece is a typical relic of the thoroughly bad old days of eighteenth-century Italian opera and is, moreover, in flagrant conflict with the composer's own new and revolutionary theories of operatic reform first exhibited in his Italian *Orfeo* (and only the da capo section of a much longer display was retained by Gluck in 1774), there is no doubt that something like it can make an exciting ending to the generally static and elegiac first act of *Orphée*. If there is to be an interval at this point in the action (in some earlier performances of the Vienna version the original three short acts were performed without a break) it is obvious that, in order to make an effective curtain in a large theatre, something more is needed than Gluck's very few bars of conventional orchestral thunder and lightning. Gluck may not have had the time or the inclination to write a new and more appropriate aria for this scene and this may help to explain why both he and, later on, Berlioz himself should have succumbed to the blandishments of their singers.

Other arias by Gluck, of a less exhibitionist nature, have been interpolated here upon occasion. The sombre 'Divinités du Styx' from *Alceste* has been pressed into service by certain singers, while Berlioz suggested that 'Ô combats! ô désordre extrême' from *Écho et Narcisse* might provide an acceptable alternative.

Finally, in order to remind ourselves of the potential which still lies hidden in Gluck's now much despised aria, let us hark back to the contemporary English music critic, Chorley, and his comments on Viardot's performance in Berlioz' adaptation of *Orphée* at the Théâtre Lyrique in Paris in 1859:

her bravura at the end of the first act showed the artist to be supreme in another light – in that grandeur of execution belonging to the old school, rapidly becoming a lost art. The torrents of roulades, the chains of notes, unmeaning in themselves, were flung out with such exactness, limitless volubility and majesty, as to convert what is essentially a commonplace piece of parade into one of those displays of passionate enthusiasm to which nothing less florid could give scope. As affording relief and contrast, they are not merely pardonable, they are defensible; and thus only to be despised by the indolence of the day, which, in obedience to false taste and narrow pedantry, has allowed one essential branch of art to fall into disuse. (Quoted in H. Pleasants, *The Great Singers* (London, 1967), p. 221)

Sic transit gloria mundi.

Hands off *Orfeo*!
BY JOHN ELIOT GARDINER

Gluck's *Orfeo ed Euridice* is acknowledged to be a masterpiece and a milestone in the history of opera, the one opera of Gluck's to have retained a regular place in the repertoire of most international opera houses. Yet even today it is scarcely known or ever performed in its original state. It has been more frequently and more drastically bowdlerised than any other work of Gluck's or indeed any opera surviving from the eighteenth century. The assaults perpetrated on the original score far outstrip, for example, the wholesale reorchestration of Rameau's operas in the *Œuvres complètes* (supervised by Saint-Saëns at the turn of this century) or the transpositions and reworkings by Oskar Hagen and other German editors of several of Handel's *opere serie* during the 1920s.

This state of affairs derives from a succession of misguided, well-meaning attempts to accommodate *Orfeo* to the prevailing tastes of the day. Those responsible for repertoire planning in our opera houses are given to arguing that Gluck will empty the theatre, the implication being that the public will only come even to such a favourite work as *Orfeo* if the opera is made to conform to what they are used to (which in effect means an approximation to a nineteenth-century operatic style). This attitude has wide-scale ramifications affecting casting, the vocal type of the hero, the pitch at which the opera is sung, the orchestration, even the length of the work. Hence the fudged compromises by those conductors and producers who think they know better than the composer and insist on imposing their own alien interpretation, regardless of whether it fits the score.

There is a curious irony in the fact that the deplorable habit of substituting a female mezzo or contralto for the hero derived from one of Gluck's most zealous supporters, Hector Berlioz. It might be claimed in defence of the distortions to which Berlioz and later editors subjected *Orfeo* during the nineteenth century that its idiom, combining an austere classicism with the use of an obsolete vocal type (the castrato) and an obsolete, characteristically baroque instrumentation, was impossibly remote from the prevailing romanticism. That is certainly not the case now. Leaving aside for the moment the problem of finding a suitable substitute for the male castrato hero, the spectacular development in historically aware performing techniques both in singing and in playing, particularly over the last ten years, makes the task of reviving such a work in close conformity to the original both feasible and intensely illuminating.

In his essay 'Handel Today', Winton Dean draws an important moral: when reviving an unfamiliar work by a great composer of the past it is asking for trouble to pull punches. If the composer is worth reviving he should be allowed to speak for himself. Gluck's *Orfeo* in its original version is still astonishingly unfamiliar: although the score has been accessible since 1963 in the excellent Urtext edition by Abert and Finscher, no corresponding orchestral material is yet available for hire or sale, to my knowledge. But when, instead of the composite version nearly always performed today, the opera is given with period instruments, historical awareness, and a male mezzo falsettist in the title role, when, in other words, Gluck's music is thrown back into a living context, then the direct, quick-striking power of the original is remarkable and indeed still revolutionary.

What makes the original version so specially eloquent and powerful and thus worthy of revival? It is hard to define its particular magic: the cumulative impact of the work is so much greater in performance than an analysis of the composite parts and means of expression would lead one to expect. It is equally difficult to apportion credit for its success, for behind the music can be felt not only the influence of Algarotti's teachings, but the active presence of the opera's choreographer Angiolini and its designer Quaglio, and the overall artistic conception of its librettist Calzabigi. Together they formed a veritable hotbed of intellectual experimenters who, between them, and at Count Durazzo's instigation, instilled revolutionary artistic ideals in the Vienna court composer. Calzabigi above all provided him, in Gluck's own words, with a drama 'composed of striking situations, exploiting those elements of terror and pathos which provide the composer with the opportunity to express great passion and to write strong and stirring music' (letter to *Mercure de France*, 1 February 1773).

Gluck rose to this occasion with music of extraordinary purity, directness and concision. Both words and music concentrate on the story of Orpheus and on every shade of feeling expressed by hero and heroine in the course of the drama. There is a complete absence of frills and self-indulgence. Part of the work's beauty lies in the fact that all individual details are subordinated to the general plan of the whole: passion is here blended with a classical spirit in an ideal balance, fulfilling the requirements of J. C. Gottsched, that 'in opera one should observe a noble simplicity [*edle Einfalt,* the phrase Winckelmann used thirty years later in his definition of classicism] rather than the sprawling excesses of the Italians' (*Kritische Dichtkunst,* III (Vienna, 1734)). Only the overture and the happy ending provide a conventionally acceptable framework to the presentation of this antique myth, and there is a view which regards the latter not as anticlimactic but as organically related to the unfolding of the plot (see above, p. 38). The plot itself, simplified to the verge of austerity, is presented as a series of tableaux rather than a connected story. Each tableau is realised as a continuous musical entity comprising a diversity of forms – chorus, dance, solo song and recitative – always appropriate to the changing moods and situations, to which Gluck's striking use of orchestral colours contributes an atmospheric depth. The forms themselves are often strongly differentiated in both key and rhythmic character, but are rigorously controlled by an overall tonal and structural plan.

This very lucidity of structure was the first casualty when Gluck himself reworked *Orfeo* for Paris in 1774. By composing extra arias for the three principals as well as additional dances, whatever their intrinsic beauty, he himself destroyed the meticulously planned balance of each act. Only four years earlier he had written that 'He who is concerned with truthfulness must model himself to his subject, and the noblest beauties of harmony and melody become serious faults if they are misplaced' (preface to *Paride ed Elena*). But his attempt to meet the Parisian appetite for *divertissement* encroached upon Calzabigi's careful construction of moods and emotions and made the characterisation of the principals generally less convincing. For example, Eurydice's new aria in Act II scene 2, 'Cet asile aimable', sung when she is strictly speaking 'dead', makes her fierce chiding of Orpheus in Act III less credible.

Accommodating *Orfeo* to Parisian tastes was damaging to it despite the fact that the very organisation of the Vienna original, while applied to an Italian musical idiom, was essentially French in origin, deriving from Calzabigi's ten-year Parisian exposure to Rameau's *tragédies lyriques* in the 1750s. By coincidence, in the very year in which Gluck first arrived in Paris – 1764 – to see his original version of *Orfeo* published, Rameau, then in his last year, and battle-scarred after spending the greater part of his creative life in trying to achieve some realisation of his musical ideals in the face of Parisian conservatism in matters of opera, was actively involved in rehearsing the last and greatest of his *tragédies lyriques, Les Boréades,* which for the first time imposed a strong tonal and structural plan on the diversity of forms which made up French classical opera. It is interesting to speculate whether, had *Les Boréades* actually seen the light of day and been performed upon the Parisian stage, Gluck would have felt compelled to submit his original *Orfeo* to such drastic revision. (Rameau died in the course of rehearsals and the work was later shelved. Its first complete concert performance was at the Queen Elizabeth Hall, London, on 19 April 1975, conducted by myself.) *Orfeo,* which had been revolutionary for Italian opera in Vienna in 1762, might have been revolutionary for French opera in Paris in 1774. But Gluck, practical man of the theatre that he was, and anxious to consolidate the recent success of his *Iphigénie en Aulide* with the Parisian public, capitulated to French conservatism in transforming *Orfeo* to *Orphée.* He himself later conceded that it would have been easier to have written six new operas than to refashion *Orfeo* in the way that he felt obliged (see Rosendorfer, 'Wer hilft dem Ritter Gluck?', p. 449).

The initial task, of course, was one of translation, which in turn led to the total recomposition of the recitatives. These certainly bear comparison with the Italian of the original version. Next came the more drastic task of adapting the music originally written for a castrato for an *haute-contre.* The transposition involved not only jettisoning the carefully judged tonal sequence of the original, it actually gave a different slant to the character of Orpheus. Whereas the castrato voice as Gluck used it with Guadagni's talents in mind emphasised the universal and mystical qualities of Orpheus as god of song, the new setting for an *haute-contre* singing at the upper extremity of his range emphasised predominantly the heroic. Contemporary accounts stress the sheer excitement of Le Gros' delivery, and thus bear witness to a very different effect from that of Guadagni's impassioned but other-worldly beauty. The very frisson created by Le Gros' singing may have prompted Gluck to develop Orpheus as a hero of action, a process that had already begun in 1769 when he transposed Orpheus's music upwards for the soprano castrato Giuseppe Millico.

Added to this, Gluck's simplification of his orchestration to fit the new circumstances of a larger auditorium involved a loss of many of the subtleties and instrumental timbres of the original, not just in 'Che puro ciel' but in the less discriminate substitution of oboes and clarinets for the more finely differentiated timbres of chalumeau, cornetto and cor anglais. 'Concerted instruments should be introduced in proportion to the interest and intensity of the words', wrote Gluck in his preface to

Alceste (1767). This precept is followed more successfully in *Orfeo* than in *Orphée*. An oboe answering a tenor at the octave in 'Chiamo il mio ben così' is a poor substitute for the perfect echoing (in timbre and pitch) of the male mezzo by a chalumeau in the Vienna version. But most of all, in passing from *Orfeo* to *Orphée*, one has the impression of musical and dramatic material extended beyond its natural dimensions. Calzabigi, in speaking of the original version, said that 'the duration is limited to what does not tire or make the attention wander' (letter of 6 March 1767, quoted in the preface to Finscher's edition, 1967). The French critic La Harpe, in comparing the two versions, spoke of *Orfeo* as a 'coherent whole, a spectacle confined within the limits of a reasonable duration, a drama holding the interest by its unity', whereas the critic of the *Mercure de France*, speaking of *Orphée*, accurately pointed out that 'the plot is surely too simple for three acts. Its uneventfulness and monotony produced tedium' (both quoted *ibid.*).

Orphée is, in effect, a separate work, couched in a new stylistic idiom, a painstaking adaptation and one which Calzabigi would scarcely have recognised, let alone condoned. To say that it represents Gluck's 'final thoughts' may be historically accurate but cannot be taken to mean that the composer was in any way dissatisfied with his original version, nor used as a serious argument for our reviving it in preference to the earlier work. To revive *Orphée* in preference to *Orfeo* is tantamount to admitting that our powers of concentration and appreciation are no better than those of the butterfly-minded Parisians of the eighteenth century. The final choice between the pulsating intensity of the original *azione teatrale* and the sensuous allure and heroic grandeur of the more heavily padded French *tragédie* turns on the particular circumstances of revival — the size of stage, auditorium and orchestra, and the availability of a satisfactory replacement in the one case for a castrato and in the other for an *haute-contre* of Le Gros' exceptional range. Both vocal types are technically speaking obsolete, the one physiologically, the other perhaps just temporarily, because of fashion. But there are undoubtedly nearer equivalents to be found nowadays than what we might call the Berlioz solution which, far from combining the 'best of both worlds', involves the use of a female Orpheus and transpositions in key, sex and character which were never sanctioned by Gluck. By playing the French version at approximately A=409, i.e. nearly a tone lower than today's pitch, one can bring Orpheus's role within the range of certain high, light tenors capable of 'mixing' the top of their voices. By substituting a male mezzo falsettist of fine sensibility, dramatic flair and powerful dynamic range (*not* a characteristically

English cathedral counter-tenor), one can find a more than satisfactory equivalent for Guadagni; and such singers do exist today.

What follows is a more subjective assessment based on two separate revivals of the original Vienna version which I conducted in concert versions in London (May 1976) and Innsbruck (August 1979). They began from the assumption that it is quite unnecessary to resort to transpositions, dilutions or substitutions to bring *Orfeo* to life, paid strict attention to Gluck's original instrumentation (which was falsified by the subsequent transposition up and down of the role of Orpheus, and also by misunderstandings arising from the careless, almost short-hand method of writing down orchestral scores in the mid eighteenth century), and led to the inescapable conclusion that *Orfeo* is a masterpiece which requires no adaptation for twentieth-century ears, once nothing is allowed to disturb or detract from the razor-sharp intensity of Gluck's vision.

In both performances the part of Orpheus was sung by the American mezzo falsettist John Angelo Messana, who combined a rare tenderness, agility and wide dynamic range in his dramatic projection of the title role. In rehearsal we endeavoured to reinstate as far as possible the known features of mid-eighteenth-century vocal style (particularly in relation to the correct interpretation of grace notes, appoggiaturas and the use of *notes inégales.*) We were fortunate in having recourse to the anthology of Italian arias (belonging to Sir Charles Mackerras) edited in 1779 in London by Domenico Corri, which contains several passages from *Orfeo* 'sung by Sigr. Guadagni' (see above, p. 58). One could not, of course, be absolutely sure that these represented the exact ornamental interpretation of Guadagni, but most of the embellishments and short cadenzas seemed sufficiently convincing to be absorbed into the vocal line and in performance gave heightened intensity to 'Chiamo il mio ben così', 'Deh! placatevi' and 'Che farò' (see above, Ex. 10, p. 58), 'A few notes with frequent pauses, and opportunities of being liberated from the composer and the band, were all [Guadagni] wanted', according to Charles Burney (*General History,* ii, p. 876).

Gluck's music, which does not seem particularly impressive in piano reduction or as 'eye music', leaps from the page in orchestral performance, especially when played by instruments of the period with accuracy, control and conviction. In the London performance a chalumeau, cornetti and narrow-bore trombones were added to conventional modern strings and woodwind; in Innsbruck a fully 'baroque' orchestra, of exactly the same size but composed entirely of period instruments, was used. The overall gain was in vividness and immediacy. There is nothing whatever 'naive or simplistic' (see above, p. 34) about Gluck's orchestration in *Orfeo*, and in performance one can admire his perfectly calculated integration of voice and instrumental accompaniment. One of the most lasting memories is of the at-pitch exchanges of Alan Hacker's plangent chalumeau echoing from a distance Messana's elegiac lament in 'Chiamo il mio ben cosi' and its linking recitatives – an almost uncanny matching of timbre and expression. Another is of the extraordinary atmosphere created by the cornetti and trombones in the opening sinfonia (the 'melancholy symphony' demanded by Calzabigi), heard first alone, then doubling the choral parts, then alone again, forming a perfect palindrome. The feeling of sombre ritual is reminiscent of much earlier music – for example, J. S. Bach employed almost identical instrumental forces in his funeral motet 'O Jesu Christ meins' Lebens Licht' (BWV 118) and in the first two verses of Cantata no. 4, 'Christ lag in Todesbanden'.

A consistent use of period instruments has the effect of immediately bringing a greater transparency of line and clearer articulation to even such a complex web of delicate sounds as Gluck's original scheme for 'Che puro ciel', in which the accompaniment moves as it were centre-stage and the declamation of the text hovers above it as a commentary (see above, Ex. 7, p. 47). The accompanied recitatives, which on modern instruments can produce that monotonous, thick, soporific sound which Berlioz rightly deplored, have extra bite and urgency when Gluck's instrumental colours are restored. 'I believed,' he wrote to Leopold of Tuscany, 'that music should achieve the same effect as lively colours and a well-balanced contrast of light and shade in a correct and well-disposed painting, so animating the figures without altering their contours' (letter written in 1767, quoted in the preface to Finscher's edition, 1967). In a faithful revival, this analogy suddenly makes sense: the juxtaposition of families of period instruments, each with its own characteristics, creates a natural and three-dimensional texture, posing none of the problems of balance that occur with modern instruments.

These evaluations are based, it is true, on the experience of concert performances. The wholesale conversion of the public to Gluck's famous masterpiece will need a determined effort, requiring a production, a true music drama, that aims for the dramatic urgency and truth so desired by Gluck and Calzabigi. In undertaking it, we should not be deterred by the knowledge that Gluck, Calzabigi, Durazzo and their circle were in their day experimenting as it were for their own satisfaction: the appeal of their avant-garde creation is universal and timeless.

Gluck and the Wagner family
BY PATRICIA HOWARD

A special contribution to the renewal of *Orfeo* in the twentieth century was made by the Wagner family. Richard Wagner had been a great Gluck enthusiast, tampering with several of Gluck's scores, reorchestrating them and adding whole new sections, so that the slender drama of *Iphigénie en Aulide* which Wagner edited in 1847, for example, was inflated into a continuous music drama on a near-Wagnerian time-scale. And the younger generations of the family seem to have felt the same need to reinterpret these works for their own time.

The twentieth-century Wagners have not been bothered by the so-called musical limitations of Gluck's scores – in this century economy and directness are not seen as handicaps – but by another characteristic of *Orfeo* in particular, and one that seems to embed it inextricably in the eighteenth century. This is the *lieto fine*, the happy ending, which has proved such a stumbling-block to so many scholars and critics, who seem obliged to excuse it on the spurious grounds that it was a consequence of the work's being designed for the emperor's name-day (though as we have shown in Chapter 3, this is untrue).

For his production at Munich on 4 March 1953, Wieland Wagner arrived at the ultimate in radical solutions to this imagined dilemma: he omitted the happy ending altogether, repeating the opening mourning chorus after 'Che farò' to bring the work to a tragic conclusion.

From Ovid to Cocteau, from the first Orpheus opera by the Italian Poliziano of 1524 through the magnificent Monteverdi to Liszt, Krenek and Stravinsky, the myth of the Thracian singer Orpheus has inspired poets and musicians again and again to artistic creation. The story of his love for Eurydice is without question a subject of real tragic force: despite the heroic constancy of his love, he is destroyed by this very love which makes him break the taboo decreed by the gods to test him. (Similar prohibitions are the causes of tragic developments for example in Biblical myths and also in the Celtic legends concerning Lohengrin.) The disregard of a divine order can only end in tragedy.

'In order to accommodate the legend to our theatre,' writes the erudite humanist Calzabigi in his preface to the Vienna version of Gluck's *Orfeo*, 'I had to transform the ending.' He therefore allows Amor, who in the first scene brings the message of the gods to Orpheus, to act as a model example of a truly baroque 'deus ex machina', to reawaken Eurydice for him and to enable the pair to experience, as a reward, the joys of marital love 'in the upper world'. This 'pleasing regard for the requirements of our local theatre' is only appreciated in a contemporary Viennese notice of 1762: 'All spectators, who otherwise would have returned to their homes saddened by shared suffering,' (we are at the beginning of the Werther period!) 'are most grateful to him for this happy change. Has virtuous Orpheus not merited a happy fate?'

This reawakening of Eurydice degrades the noble work of Gluck to a 'jest' arranged by Amor, whereas the original myth expresses in the most pregnant manner the existential perception that in life there can be no turning back. Significantly, the music of the great dramatist is of a timeless validity exactly until the start of the 'accommodated' ending, which turns into a typical baroque flourish in the 'official' D major tonality (with trumpets and timpani!). This ending is only acceptable to our present-day sensibility in a strictly historicising performance, which would be of as little service to Gluck as to any other music-dramatic genius.

The casting of the title role has always been a controversial problem. It is well known that Gluck wrote the part of Orpheus for the famous castrato Guadagni, but later recast it for tenor in order to make possible a Paris performance. Franz Liszt used a tenor in 1854 at Weimar, while Berlioz arranged his 1859 version for the contralto of Viardot-Garcia. Since the beginning of the nineteenth century Orpheus was sung in Germany by a contralto. A male casting of the part inevitably introduces an element of sensuality into the work which is alien to it. In this new production Orpheus is deliberately given to a contralto, whilst the ending used may be regarded as controversial. It reverts to the original legend, as Toscanini did in his production at the Metropolitan, but without borrowing musical fragments from other works of Gluck as he did.

The bereavement of Orpheus, his defiance, his prevailing and his defeat are presented by Gluck with an almost ascetic avoidance of all operatic hyperbole and an unusual concentration of the action entirely in the spirit of antique tragedy. His music conveys powerful intensity and, at the same time, tenderest lyricism. It is, despite its age, 'musica viva' in the truest sense. For the musician and the producer, *Orpheus,* because of its structure probably best described as a 'lyric tragedy', constitutes a special stylistic problem. Equidistant from the style of Handel and that of Mozart, a different style will have to be found for the performance of Gluck which can keep his work alive in the German theatre of the present and future.

(Wieland Wagner, 'Zur Neuinszenierung des Orpheus',
Blätter der Bayerischen Staatsoper, 5/7
(1952-3), pp. 107-8, trans.
Hans Heimler).

Such an act of musical vandalism was unlikely to gain many converts, and I have not been able to trace any subsequent productions of this version of the opera. It has, however, been the work of another Wagner which has marked the next step in the recreation of *Orfeo* for our century.

While the score of the opera has provided an almost irresistible invitation to conductors and editors to update and adapt it, with the precedent of the composer's own reworking apparently authorising such changes, producers have on the whole caused little stir. Few productions have ventured away from an evocation of the classical world: costumes more or less Greek, scenery of the simplest in either a representational or a symbolic mould. The story offers an important role for lighting, but even here, subtleties seem to be precluded by the elemental simplicity of the story. So deeply rooted is this convention of a classical production that any departure from it is bound to shock.

It seems clear that Wolf Siegfried Wagner's production at Wexford on 20 October 1977 was a deliberately calculated shock. But it is equally evident that the producer was more concerned to provoke sensations of outrage than to reveal a new interpretation of the opera. The cast who worked with him are still unsure of the meaning of all his symbols, though we can deduce that the *lieto fine* was, once more, an issue that this Wagner found difficult to incorporate into a tragic myth, and his solution, at once sensual and trivial, reflects his unease as clearly as does Wieland's butchery. However, an urgent sense of recreation, of bringing the opera forcibly back to a new life – a not inappropriate treatment of the drama of Orpheus – infused his remarkable production, and has perhaps opened up the way for less reverent treatments of what Calzabigi felt to be an enduringly relevant myth.

To balance the few and valuable eye-witness accounts of Gluck and his singers included in the earlier chapters, this production is here described by Kevin Smith.

The *Orfeo* show
BY KEVIN SMITH

I walked through the passport control at Heathrow airport with rather more on my mind than collecting my luggage. I was, in fact, eager to discover whether I would be singing, later in the year, one of the most sought-after roles in the history of opera. Some weeks before, I had been asked to audition for the role of Orpheus in Gluck's opera, which was to be produced at the Wexford Festival, and now on my return to London I waited impatiently for my agent to answer my telephone call. The news was good. The audition had been successful. The contract had arrived and was awaiting my signature.

Sometime later, when the elation had subsided somewhat, I began to be aware of what I had taken on. Firstly, I would be, as far as I knew, the first counter-tenor to perform this role in a staged production at the pitch at which it was originally conceived. Secondly, I would be following in the steps of a galaxy of famous singers who had sung this coveted part, such as Alexander Young, Dietrich Fischer-Dieskau, Marilyn Horne, Teresa Berganza, Janet Baker and of course the contralto who is best remembered for her portrayal of Orpheus, Kathleen Ferrier. Thirdly, the very fact that I was a counter-tenor would no doubt spark off the usual objections regarding the suitability of the counter-tenor voice on the operatic stage.

Arguments against the use of the voice have included suggestions that it lacks volume, that it is not dramatic and, in the case of baroque opera, that it is totally different in timbre from what had originally been intended. To answer the first objections it is only necessary to look back over the last few years and note that more operas are being performed with counter-tenors in prominent roles, and I am quite convinced that opera houses such as Covent Garden and the Coliseum in London, the Opéra in Paris, and theatres in Hamburg, Zurich, Vienna, San Francisco and Buenos Aires, to name but a few, would not countenance employing a counter-tenor if he was inaudible or if his voice was lacking in dramatic intensity. With regard to the difference in timbre between the modern counter-tenor and the castrato of old, there can be no one around today who is in a position to compare the sound. That there is a difference is not in dispute. But whether the counter-tenor is better or worse than his predecessor can only be matter for conjecture. In my opinion, if a counter-tenor is able to perform an operatic role originally written for a castrato with both musical and dramatic conviction, then why on earth shouldn't he? The first performer of the role of Orpheus was a contralto castrato, Gaetano Guadagni, and the tessitura of the 1762 version is ideally suited to a modern counter-tenor, having a range of an octave and a fifth, that is from the A below middle C to the octave E above.

During the last few weeks of September I managed to meet Jane Glover, the conductor, two or three times in order that we might both have some idea of each other's musical approach to the work. I also met Alex Reid for a costume fitting. He had designed a superb costume for me – eighteenth century, not classical – in silver, grey and white, and I was very pleased that I would be so well dressed.

I was particularly looking forward to meeting the producer, Wolf Siegfried Wagner, since from the very first discussions in London his name had been spoken of as though he were some mysterious figure from one of his great-grandfather's operas. I had heard amazing rumours of his plans for *Orfeo*. It was said that he would upset many people. It was not to be a production in the traditional manner, but would be full of modernistic gimmicks. There was dark talk of hypodermic syringes, drugs, motor bikes and even nudity. It seemed that even before the first day of rehearsal, the *'Orfeo* show' had the makings of being the *enfant terrible* of the festival.

At my first meeting with Herr Wagner I casually asked him about his ideas for the opera. He replied that he had quite a few. He then showed me the set design, an intriguing one by Dacre Punt. It consisted of a backcloth on which was projected an architectural engraving, the perspective of which was so deceptive to the eye that it left the viewer totally confused as to whether he was vertical or horizontal. The wings of the stage and the proscenium arch were covered with mirrors. In a review in the *Spectator* on 29 October 1977, Rodney Milnes described the set as an 'eighteenth century architectural caprice with all planes going in every direction at once,' and concluded, 'this was maybe not a show to see with a drink or two on board'.

I then asked Herr Wagner how he saw the role of Orpheus in his production. He didn't answer directly but smiled secretively, and then said that he thought Orpheus was a dreamer. At this point our conversation was interrupted by a telephone call. As he left, he turned and asked me conspiratorially whether I had ever taken any hard drugs. Before I had time to reply, he had gone – leaving me with the thought that perhaps all the rumours rife in Wexford were true after all. Good God, did he want me to portray Orpheus as a junkie?

On Wednesday 13 October we had our first complete run-through: a chaotic affair. Words and music, known perfectly at ten o'clock, came tumbling out in any order an hour later. Moves which had been carefully plotted were late, early, or didn't happen at all. Nevertheless, in spite of the problems I could see the pattern of the production falling into place, and I felt that at last progress was being made. Until this point I had felt like a puppet, with Wagner moving the strings. It was obviously his intention to outrage the audience by introducing bizarre modern symbols into each scene, and although he at no time explained his approach to the cast, or enlightened us as to the meaning of any of his startling symbols, I became aware that his approach showed a deep understanding of the motivation and development of each character, and of the overall shape of the drama.

The public dress rehearsal of *Orfeo* was scheduled for 18 October, and here was our first opportunity to work in front of a large group of people. It gave us the possibility of gauging the audience's reaction to the production. We could also probe the atmosphere created by the

drama — those indescribable sensations which flow from stage to auditorium and back, so vital to any performer.

In spite of the fact that our front curtain was missing and the lighting plot was incomplete, we had a most successful run-through with few mishaps. Our audience did not seem to be intimidated by Herr Wagner's 'eccentricities', and took the unconventional production very much in its stride. There were some embarrassed titters during a dance sequence when two of the ballet appeared in see-through body stockings, but otherwise all went well.

The first night was more eventful. Shortly before curtain-up I heard a very loud thud from the stage: the rope which held up a large and heavy glitter ball, which appeared in Act II, had broken, and rope and ball dropped some twenty feet to the stage, narrowly missing John Cruikshank, our stage manager, who had been underneath. The front cloth, which had been delayed in customs, had arrived only hours before, and was being hung in some haste. The sprightly overture began. As the first chorus followed it, the curtain went up — or rather it was more of a sideways motion accompanied by an ominous ripping sound. The cloth had caught in a lighting bar and torn itself from top to bottom on one side. The gasps from the audience were followed by a loud guffaw and laughter as Eurydice's resting place came into view. It had more in common with a perspex shower enclosure than a traditional coffin, and contained a number of heart-shaped balloons which bobbed aimlessly about in every direction. In her review for the *Financial Times* (31 October 1977) Elizabeth Forbes wrote, 'Eurydice's remains — there has obviously been an autopsy — float in a glass tank of formaldehyde.'

During the first scene of Act II, Orpheus pleads with the Furies to allow him into Elysium, in order that he may continue his search for Eurydice. I always enjoyed singing the impassioned vocal line, and the hidden singers behind the backcloth seemed to revel in their emphatic choruses. It was at the end of the scene that I was captured by the balletic Furies, dragged to the back of the stage and positioned directly underneath the ten-foot-long hypodermic syringe which, swathed in flashing neon lights, descended threateningly upon me. This episode brought forth groans and laughter in equal amounts from various parts of the audience, reactions which subsided as the syringe was flown out, only to break out afresh at the appearance of the (now rehung) glitter globe. For a while, the opening music of 'Che puro ciel' was obscured. However, Gluck's marvellous music managed to calm not only the Furies but the audience too, and I was allowed to complete the aria without interruption. Then followed a charming ballet, and Act II closed as, with face averted, I prepared to lead my beloved Eurydice back to the world of the living.

The final act began with Orpheus and Eurydice in the same pose as at the end of Act II, but with an enormous black metronome at the back of the stage, with an eye on its inverted pendulum, which swung silently from side to side. Jennifer Smith (Eurydice) and I began singing the energetic exchanges which precede the dramatic duet. Then came Eurydice's one stunning aria, 'Che fiero momento', full of bitter despair. There was at this point a most intense atmosphere in the theatre which held through Eurydice's death (when the metronome stopped, symbolically) until the end of the famous lament 'Che farò', when there was enthusiastic applause. Grateful as I was for this, I would have preferred to continue the dramatic intensity through the next recitative, where Orpheus describes his grief and his desire to be united in death with his wife.

It was here that Gluck and Calzabigi changed the outcome of the myth in order that the opera might end happily. It was also here that our producer decided to close his production in a vaudeville style. The performance ended with the three singers – Orpheus, Eurydice and Cupid – perched on a large lip-shaped red sofa ('no awards for guessing what *that* symbolises', wrote Elizabeth Forbes), around which the dancers placed museum ropes as though we were some ancient exhibit. Wagner could have found no clearer way of showing what he thought of the convention of the happy ending.

There was no doubt that the evening had been a success. The hecklers were drowned by the enthusiastic applause. Arguments for and against the production continued throughout the festival, and Herr Wagner had obviously achieved what he must have intended – a highly entertaining and yet challenging and sensitive reinterpretation of one of the most famous operas of all time. I left Wexford with a deep admiration for everyone who had been involved in the '*Orfeo* show'.

9 Table of numbers

COMPILED BY EVE BARSHAM

The following table of numbers is based on the 1762 *Orfeo* (published in 1764), the 1774 *Orphée* (published in that year) and Berlioz' 1859 version (published in 1866). 'R' and 'N' against items in the 1774 score denote that the music was rewritten (R) or was altogether new (N). 'C' alongside items in the 1866 score indicates changes (other than key changes) in comparison with the corresponding item in the 1774 score.

There are a few borrowings from earlier works by Gluck in both *Orfeo* and *Orphée*. In the former, the aria 'Che puro ciel' (Act II) is taken from the operas *Ezio* (1750) and *Antigono* (1756). The ballet in B flat in the same act is taken from an aria in *Demofoonte* (1743). In *Orphée*, the aria 'L'espoir renaît dans mon âme' (Act I) is taken from *Le feste d'Apollo* (1769) and *Il Parnasso confuso* (1765). The Furies' dance in Act II is taken from the finale of the ballet *Don Juan* (1761) and the gavotte from *Paride ed Elena* (1770). At the end of Act III, the trio 'Tender Amour' is also taken from *Paride ed Elena*. The *air vif* and the following minuet are from the overture to *Il trionfo di Clelia* (1763), and the chaconne from *Iphigénie en Aulide* (1774).

The duration of the opera is comparatively brief, playing for only about 110 minutes in the French version and a bare ninety minutes in the Italian.

The orchestra in the score published in 1764 comprises two flutes, two chalumeaux, two oboes, two cors anglais, two bassoons, two cornetti, two horns, two trumpets, three trombones, timpani, harp, strings and harpsichord.

In the 1774 score the orchestra consists of two flutes, two oboes, two clarinets, two bassoons, two horns, two trumpets, three trombones, timpani, harp and strings.

Berlioz' score of 1866 calls for two flutes, two oboes, two cors anglais, two clarinets, two bassoons, two horns, two trumpets, cornet, three trombones, timpani, harp and strings.

1764	1774	1866
Act I scene 1	**Act I scene 1**	**Act I scene 1**
Ov Overture (C major)	Ov Overture (C major)	Ov Overture (C major)
1 Chorus and Orfeo: 'Ah se intorno' (C minor)	1 Chorus and Orphée: 'Ah! dans ce bois!' (C minor) R	1 Chorus and Orphée: 'Ah! dans ce bois' (C minor)
2 Orfeo: recitative, 'Basta, basta' (Eb major – C minor)	2 Orphée: recitative, 'Vos plaintes' (C minor – G minor)	2 Orphée: recitative, 'Vos plaintes' (C minor – G minor)
3 Ballet (Eb major)	3 Ballet (Eb major)	3 Ballet (Eb major)
4 Chorus: 'Ah se intorno' and ritornello (C minor)	4 Chorus: 'Ah! dans ce bois' (C minor)	4 Chorus: 'Ah! dans ce bois' (C minor)
	5 Orphée: recitative, 'Éloignez vous' (C minor) R	5 Orphée: recitative, 'Éloignez vous' (C minor) C
	6 Ritornello (C minor)	6 Ritornello (C minor)
	Act I scene 2	**Act I scene 2**
5i Orfeo: aria (verse 1), 'Chiamo il mio ben cosi' (F major)	7i Orphée: aria (verse 1), 'Objet de mon amour' (C major)	7i Orphée: aria (verse 1), 'Objet de mon amour' (F major)
5ii Orfeo: recitative, 'Euridice' (F minor – C major)	7ii Orphée: recitative, 'Euridice' (C minor – G minor) R	7ii Orphée: recitative, 'Euridice' (C minor)
5iii Orfeo: aria (verse 2), 'Cerco il mio ben' (F major)	7iii Orphée: aria (verse 2), 'Accablé de regrets' (C major)	7iii Orphée: aria (verse 2), 'Accablé de regrets' (F major)

1764	1774	1866
5iv Orfeo: recitative, 'Euridice' (F major)	7iv Orphée: recitative, 'Euridice' (C major) R	7iv Orphée: recitative, 'Euridice' (F major)
5v Orfeo: aria (verse 3), 'Piango il mio ben' (F major)	7v Orphée: aria (verse 3), 'Plein de trouble' (C major)	7v Orphée: aria (verse 3), 'Plein de trouble' (F major)
6 Orfeo: recitative, 'Numi, barbari!' (G minor – A minor)	8 Orphée: recitative, 'Divinités de l'Acheron' (G minor – A minor) R	8 Orphée: recitiative, 'Divinités de l'Acheron' (D minor – E minor)
Act I scene 2	**Act I scene 3**	**Act I scene 3**
7 Orfeo, Amor: recitative, 'T'assiste Amore!' (E minor – D major)	9 Amour: recitative, 'L'Amour vient' (E minor – F major)	9 Amour: recitative, 'L'Amour vient' (E minor – F major)
	10 Amour: aria, 'Si les doux accords' (F major) N	10 Amour: aria, 'Si les doux accords' (F major)
	11 Orphée, Amour: recitative, 'Dieux! Je la reverrais!' (B♭ major – D major) R	11 Orphée, Amour: recitative, 'Dieux! Je la reverrais!' (B♭ major— D major)
8 Amor: aria, 'Gli sguardi' (G major)	12 Amour: aria, 'Soumis au silence' (G major)	12 Amour: aria, 'Soumis au silence' (G major)
9 Orfeo: recitative, 'Che disse?' (C major – D major)	13 Orphée: recitative, 'Impitoyables Dieux' (D major) R	13 Orphée: recitative, 'Qu'entends-je?' (G major – D major)
10 Orchestral coda	14 Orphée: arietta,	14 Orphée: aria,

1764	1774	1866
(D major)	'L'espoir renaît dans mon âme' (B♭ major) N	'Amour, viens rendre' (G major)
Act II scene 1	**Act II scene 1**	**Act II scene 1**
11 Ballet (E♭ major)	15 Ballet (E♭ major)	15 Ballet (E♭ major)
12i Harp prelude	16 Harp prelude	16i Harp prelude
12ii Chorus of Furies: 'Chi mai dell' Erebo'	17 Chorus of Furies: 'Quel est l'audacieux'	16ii Chorus of Furies: 'Quel est l'audacieux'
13 Ballet (C minor)	18 Ballet (D minor)	16iii Ballet (C minor)
14 Chorus of Furies: 'Chi mai dell' Erebo' (C minor)	19 Chorus of Furies: 'Quel est l'audacieux' (D minor)	17 Chorus of Furies: 'Quel est l'audacieux' (C minor)
15 Ballet (E♭ major)		
16 Harp prelude, Orfeo, Chorus: 'Deh! placatevi' (E♭ major)	20 Harp prelude, Orphée, Chorus: 'Laissez vous toucher' (B♭ major) R	18 Harp prelude, Orphée, Chorus: 'Laissez vous toucher' (E♭ major) C
17 Chorus of Furies: 'Misero giovane' (E♭ major)	21 Chorus of Furies: 'Qui t'amène' (B♭ major)	19 Chorus of Furies: 'Qui t'amène' (E♭ major)
18 Orfeo: aria, 'Mille pene' (F minor – C minor)	22 Orphée: aria, 'Ah! la flamme' (F minor – C minor) (Gluck added 3 bars in 1774)	20 Orphée: aria, 'Ah! la flamme' (C minor)
19 Chorus of Furies: 'Ah, quale incognito' (F minor)	23 Chorus of Furies: 'Par quels puissants' (G minor)	21 Chorus of Furies: 'Par quels puissants' (F minor)
20 Orfeo: aria, 'Men tiranne' (F minor)	24 Orphée: aria, 'La tendresse' (C minor)	22 Orphée: aria, 'La tendresse' (F minor)

1764	1774	1866
21 Chorus of Furies: 'Ah, quale incognito' (F minor)	25 Chorus of Furies: 'Quels chants doux' (F minor)	23 Chorus of Furies: 'Quels chants doux' (F minor)
	26 Furies' dance (D minor) N	24 Furies' dance (D minor)
Act II scene 2	**Act II scene 2**	**Act II scene 2**
22 Ballet (F major)	27i, Ballet ii, (F major – iii D minor – F major) (Gluck added the D minor section in 1774)	25i, Ballet ii, (F major – iii D minor – F major)
	28 Ballet (C major) N	26 Ballet (C major)
	29, Euridice, 30 Chorus: 'Cet asile aimable' and ritornello (F major) N	27, Euridice, 28 Chorus: 'Cet asile aimable' and ritornello (F major)
	Act II scene 3	**Act II scene 3**
23 Orfeo, Chorus: 'Che puro ciel' (C major)	31 Orphée: arioso, 'Quel nouveau ciel' (C major) R	29 Orphée: arioso, 'Quel nouveau ciel' (C major)
		Act II scene 4
24 Chorus: 'Vieni a' regni' (F major)	32 Chorus: 'Viens dans ce séjour' (F major)	30 Chorus: 'Viens dans ce séjour' (F major)
25 Ballet (Bb major)	33 Ballet (Bb major)	31 Ballet (Bb major)
26 Orfeo, Chorus: 'Anime avventurose' (E minor – C major)	34 Orphée, Chorus: 'O vous ombres' (G minor – C major)	32 Orphée, Chorus: 'O vous ombres' (G minor – C major)

1764	1774	1866
	Act II scene 4	**Act II scene 5**
27 Chorus: 'Torna, o bella' (F major)	35 Chorus: 'Près du tendre objet' (F major) (Gluck added 1 bar in 1774)	33 Chorus: 'Près du tendre objet' (F major)
Act III scene 1	**Act III scene 1**	**Act III scene 1**
28 Orfeo, Euridice: recitative, 'Vieni, segui' (F minor – D major)	36 Orphée, Euridice: recitative, 'Viens, viens' (F minor) R	34 Orphée, Euridice: recitative, 'Viens, viens' (F minor – C major)
29 Orfeo, Euridice: duet, 'Vieni, appaga' (G major)	37 Orphée, Euridice: duet, 'Viens, suis un époux' (F major)	35 Orphée, Euridice: duet, 'Viens, suis un époux' (F major)
30 Euridice: recitative, 'Qual vita' (D major – C minor)	38 Euridice: recitative, 'Mais d'où vient' (G minor – C minor) R	36 Euridice: recitative, 'Mais d'où vient' (G minor – C minor)
31 Euridice: aria, 'Che fiero momento' (C minor)	39i, Euridice, ii, Orphée: aria – iii duet – aria, 'Fortune ennemie' (C minor – E♭ major – C minor) R	37 Euridice, Orphée: aria – duet – aria, 'Fortune ennemie' (C minor – E♭ major – C minor)
32 Orfeo, Euridice: recitative, 'Ecco un nuovo tormento' (E♭ major – C major)	40 Orphée, Euridice: recitative, 'Quelle épreuve' (E♭ major – D minor) R	38 Orphée, Euridice: recitative, 'Quelle épreuve' (E♭ major – A minor)

1764	1774	1866
33 Orfeo: aria, 'Che farò senza Euridice' (C major)	41 Orphée: aria 'J'ai perdu mon Euridice' (F major) (Gluck added 3 bars in 1774)	39 Orphée: aria, 'J'ai perdu mon Euridice' (C major)
34 Orfeo: recitative, 'Ah! finisca' (D minor – F♯ minor)	42 Orphée: recitative, 'Ah! puisse ma douleur' (B♭ major – G minor) R	40 Orphée: recitative, 'Ah! puisse ma douleur' (F major – C minor)
Act III scene 2	**Act III scene 2**	**Act III scene 2**
35 Amor, Orfeo, Euridice: recitative, 'Orfeo! che fai?' (C♯ minor – D major)	43 Amour, Orphée, Euridice: recitative, 'Arrête, Orphée' (D minor – G minor)	41 Amour, Orphée, Euridice: recitative, 'Arrête, Orphée' (D minor – G minor)
Act III scene 3	**Act III scene 3**	**Act III scene 3**
	44 Chorus: 'L'Amour triomphe' (A major) R	42 Chorus: 'L'Amour triomphe' (D major)
36 Ballet: Maestoso (D major)		
37i Dolce (A major)	45i Ballet: Gracieux (A major)	43i Ballet: Grazioso (A major)
37ii Allegro (A minor)	ii Gavotte (A minor)	ii Gavotte (A minor)
	iii Air vif (C major) N	iii Ballet (C major)
	iv Menuet (C major) N	iv Menuet (C major)

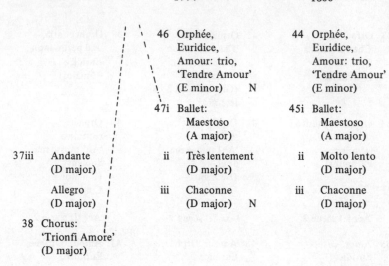

1764		1774		1866
		46 Orphée, Euridice, Amour: trio, 'Tendre Amour' (E minor) N		44 Orphée, Euridice, Amour: trio, 'Tendre Amour' (E minor)
		47i Ballet: Maestoso (A major)		45i Ballet: Maestoso (A major)
37iii Andante (D major)		ii Très lentement (D major)		ii Molto lento (D major)
Allegro (D major)		iii Chaconne (D major) N		iii Chaconne (D major)
38 Chorus: 'Trionfi Amore' (D major)				

Select bibliography

Abert, A. A. *Gluck*. Munich, 1959
Algarotti, Francesco *Saggio sopra l'opera in musica*. Leghorn, 1755
Barzun, J. *Berlioz and the Romantic Century*, 3rd edn. New York, 1969
Berlioz, Hector *Correspondance générale*, ed. P. Citron, I. Paris, 1972
    (trans. H. Searle, *Hector Berlioz, a Selection from his Letters*,
    London, 1966)
    Mémoires. Paris, 1870 (trans. D. Cairns, London, 1969)
    Les soirées de l'orchestre. Paris, 1852 (trans. J. Barzun, Chicago,
    1973)
    Traité d'instrumentation et d'orchestration. Paris, 1844 (trans. M. C.
    Clarke, 2nd edn, London, 1858)
    À travers chants. Paris, 1862 (trans. E. Evans, *Gluck and his Operas*,
    London [1915]) [quotations in the text are partly adapted from
    this translation]
Burney, Charles *General History of Music*. London, 1782-9
    The Present State of Music in Germany. London, 1775. Ed. P. Scholes,
    Dr Burney's Musical Tours in Europe, II. London, 1959
Calzabigi, Ranieri de *Dissertazione*. Paris, 1755
Casanova, G. *Mémoires*, ed. R. Abirached and E. Zorzi. Tours, 1958
Corri, Domenico *A Select Collection of the Most Admired Songs, Duetts
    etc. from Operas in the Highest Esteem*. London, 1779
    The Singer's Preceptor. London, 1810
Cumberland, Richard *Memoirs*. London, 1806
Dean, Winton 'Handel Today', *Handel and the Fitzwilliam*, ed. J.
    Huskinson. Cambridge, 1974.
Desnoiresterres, Gustave *Gluck et Piccinni*. Paris, 1875
Einstein, Alfred, trans. F. Blom *Gluck*. London, 1936
Fitzlyon, April *The Price of Genius: a Life of P. Viardot*. London, 1964
Genlis, Stephanie, Comtesse de *Mémoires inédits*. Paris, 1825
Gluck Jahrbuch ed. H. Abert, 1-4. Leipzig, 1913-18
Grimm, Melchior *Correspondance littéraire*. Paris, 1774
Haas, Robert *Gluck und Durazzo im Burgtheater*. Leipzig, 1925 [in-
    cludes the only pubd extracts relating to *Orfeo* from Count
    Zinzendorf's Journal]
Hammelmann, Hans, and Rose, Michael 'New Light on Calzabigi and
    Gluck', *Musical Times*, 110 (1969), 609-11
Heartz, Daniel 'From Garrick to Gluck: the Reform of Theatre and

Opera in the Mid Eighteenth Century', *Proceedings of the Royal Musical Association*, 94 (1967-8), 111-27

Hedgcock, Frank *David Garrick and his French Friends.* London, 1912

Heriot, Angus *The Castrati in Opera.* London, 1956

Journal de Paris. Paris, 1777-1827

Journal des Beaux-Arts. Paris, 1768-75

Kelly, Michael *Reminiscences.* London, 1826

La Laurencie, Lionel de *Orphée de Gluck.* Paris, 1934

Le Blond, G. M. *Mémoires pour servir à l'histoire de la révolution opérée dans la musique par M. le Chevalier Gluck.* Paris, 1781

Loewenberg, Alfred 'Gluck's *Orfeo* on the Stage', *Musical Quarterly,* 26 (1940), 311-39

Mannlich, Christian von *Ein deutscher Maler und Hofmann.* Berlin, 1910

Mercure de France. Paris, 1724-91

Metastasio, Pietro *Lettere.* Florence, 1787-9

Mueller von Asow, H. and E. H. *The Collected Correspondence and Papers of Christoph Willibald Gluck.* London, 1962

Noverre, J.-G. *Lettres sur la danse et sur les ballets.* Paris, 1760

Prod'homme, J.-G. *Gluck.* Paris, 1948

'Deux collaborateurs italiens de Gluck', *Rivista Musicale Italiana,* 23 (1916), 33-65

Revue de Paris. Paris, 1829-94

Rolland, Romain *Musiciens d'autrefois.* Paris, 1908 (trans. Mary Blaiklock, London 1915)

Voyage musical aux pays du passé. Paris, 1919

Rosendorfer, H. 'Wer hilft dem Ritter Gluck?', *Neue Zeitschrift für Musik,* 123 (1962)

Sternfeld, F. W. 'Expression and Revision in Gluck's *Orfeo* and *Alceste',* *Essays presented to Egon Wellesz,* ed. J. Westrup. Oxford, 1966

Viardot-Garcia, P. 'Letters to Julius Rietz' (trans. T. Baker), *Musical Quarterly,* 2 (1916), 32-59

Walterhausen, W. von *Orpheus und Eurydice.* Munich, 1923

Zinzendorf, Karl *see* Haas

Scores

Orfeo ed Euridice (1764 edition) ed. A. A. Abert and L. Finscher. Kassel, 1963 (Bärenreiter)

Orphée et Euridice (1774 edition) ed. L. Finscher. Kassel, 1967 (Bärenreiter)

Orphée et Euridice (Berlioz' edition) ed. A. Dörfell. Leipzig, 1866 (Heinze)

Alceste Vienna, 1769 (Giovanni Tomaso de Trattnern)

Paride ed Elena Vienna, 1770 (Giovanni Tomaso de Trattnern)

Discography

BY MALCOLM WALKER

O Orfeo/Orphée   ⓜ mono recording
A Amor/Amour   ⓔ electronically reprocessed stereo
E Euridice   *not generally available at present

All recordings are 33⅓ rpm in stereo unless otherwise stated; dates are those of recording

The figures in italics refer to the editions of the opera analysed in the table of numbers (above, pp. 127-34). The numbers following indicate the musical items included, in the order in which they are played

1936   (excerpts – in French) *1866:* 1, 2, 3, 5, 7 (i, iii), 10-13; *1764:* 9; *1774:* 26 (abbreviated); *1866:* 18, 19, 22, 23, 25 (ii, iii), 29 (abbreviated), 37, 38 (part), 40, 44 (abbreviated), 41; Raveau *O;* Delille *A;* Féraldy *E*/Vlassof Choir, SO/Tomasi
                       Vox (US) ⓜ OPX200*

1947   (excerpts – in Italian) *1866:* 1, 2, 6, 7 (iv, v), 8-10, 11 (abbreviated), 12 (abbreviated), 13, 15, 17, 18, 19 (abbreviated), 20-3, 33-7, 38 (abbreviated), 39, 40, 44 (abbreviated), 41; *1764:* 36, 38 (part); Ferrier *O;* Vlachopoulos *A;* Ayars *E*/Glyndebourne Festival Chorus, Southern PO/Stiedry
                       Decca ⓜ ACL293
                       London ⓜ LL5103*

1951   (live performance – in Italian) *1866:* Ov, 1-13; *1764:* 10; *1866:* 24, 15-40, 44, 45 (i, abbreviated); *1764:* 36, 38 (part); Ferrier *O;* Duval *A;* Koeman *E*/Netherlands Opera Chorus and Orch/ Bruck
                       EMI ⓜ RLS725

1951   (live performance – in Italian) Barbieri *O;* Gabory *A;* Gueden *E*/La Scala Chorus and Orch/Furtwängler
                       Cetra ⓜ LO19/2
                       Turnabout (US) ⓜ THS65112-3

1952   (Act II: live performance – in Italian) *1866:* 15-33; Merriman *O;* Gibson *E*/Shaw Chorale, NBC SO/Toscanini
                       RCA (UK) ⓜ AT127
                       (US) ⓜ LVT1041*

1953   (excerpts – in Italian) Stevens *O;* Berger *E*/RCA Victor SO/ Reiner   RCA (US) ⓜLM9010 *

137

1953   (in Italian) *1866:* Ov, 1-13; *1764:* 10; *1866:* 15-25, 27-39; *1764:*
36, 38 (part); *1866:* 43 (ii), 44, 45 (ii, iii); Klose *O;* Streich *A;*
Berger *E*/Berlin State Opera Chorus and Orch/Rother
Acanta ⓜ FA22140
Urania (US) ⓔ US5223/3*

1954   (excerpts – in German) *1866:* Ov, 7 (i, iv, v), 12, 24-30, 39;
Klose *O:* Streich *A;* Schlemm *E*/Bavarian Radio Chorus, Berlin
RIAS SO, Munich PO/Rother
DG ⓜ 478128

1954   (in Russian) *1774:* Ov, 1-13; *1764:* 10; *1774:* 15-35, 36 (abbre-
viated), 37-42, 45 (i-iii); Kozlovsky *O;* Sakharova *A;* Shumskaya
E/USSR Radio Chorus and Orch/Samosud
MK ⓜ DO933-40

1955   (in French) *1774:* Ov, 1-6, 7 (i-iv), 8-13, 26, 15-25, 27-31, 33,
34, 32, 35-42, 45 (i, ii, iv – abbreviated), 46, 47 (ii, iii – abbreviated); Gedda *O;* Berton *A;* Micheau *E*/Paris Conservatoire
Chorus and Orch/Froment
EMI ⓜ 2C 153 12059-60

1956   (in French) *1774:* Ov, 1-13; *1764:* 10; *1774:* 15-42, 46, 45, (i,
ii, iv), 44; Simoneau *O;* Alarie *A;* Danco *E*/Blanchard Vocal
Ensemble, Lamoureux Orch/Rosbaud
Philips ⓜ PHC2-014*

1956   (in Italian) *1866:* Ov, 1-13; *1774:* 10; *1866:* 15-25 (ii, iii), 27-
30, 32-40; *1764:* 36, 38 (part); Stevens *O;* Peters *A;* Della Casa
E/Rome Opera Chorus and Orch/Monteux
RCA (UK) ⓜ RB16058-60*
(US) ⓜ LM6136*

1960   (excerpts – in German) *1866:* 1, 7-12, 17, 18 (abbreviated), 23,
24, 25 (i), 27, 32, 34, 35, 37 (abbreviated), 38 (abbreviated),
39, 40; *1764:* 36, 38 (part); Prey *O;* Köth *A;* Lorengar *E*/Berlin
Chamber Choir, Berlin SO/Stein
EMI 1C 063 28505

1965   (in Italian) *1866:* Ov, 1-13; *1764:* 10; *1866:* 15-40; *1764:* 36,
38 (part); *1866:* 43-5; Verrett *O;* Raskin *A;* Moffo *E*/Rome
Polyphonic Choir, Virtuosi di Roma and Instrumental Ensemble
of Collegium Musicum Italicum/Fasano
RCA (UK) SER5539-41
(UK) LSC6169

1966   (in Italian) *1764:* Ov, 1-15; *1866:* 18; *1764:* 17-21; *1774:* 26,
27 (i-iii), 29-30; *1764:* 23-32; *1866:* 33; *1764:* 34-8; Forrester
O; Steffek *A;* Stich-Randall *E*/Vienna Academy Choir, Vienna
State Opera Orch/Mackerras
Vanguard (US) VSD70686-7
EMI 1C 147 98121-2

1966   (in Italian) *1764:* Ov, 1-14, 16-36, 37 (i-iv abbreviated), 38;
Bumbry *O;* Pütz *A;* Rothenberger *E*/Leipzig Radio Chorus,
Leipzig Gewandhaus Orch/Neumann
EMI SMA91602-3*
Angel SBL3717*

1967 (in Italian) *1764:* Ov, 1-14; *1774:* 26; *1764:* 15-36, 37 (i, iii, iv), 38; Fischer-Dieskau *O;* Moser *A;* Janowitz *E*/Munich Bach Choir and Orch/Richter

DG 2726 043

1969 (in Italian) *1764:* Ov, 1; *1866:* 2; *1774:* 3; *1764:* 4, 5 (i, iii, v: recitatives from *1866,* 7ii, 7iv), 6; *1866:* 8-14; *1764:* 11-15; *1866:* 22; *1764:* 17; *1866:* 20; *1764:* 19-21; *1866:* 20; *1764:* 19-21; *1774:* 16, 27 (i-iii); *1866:* 27-9; *1764:* 24, 26-30, 31 (part one; part two from *1866,* 35; *da capo* from *1764,* 31), 32 (part one; part two from *1866,* 38); *1866:* 39 (orchestral coda from *1764,* 33); *1764:* 34-5; *1866:* 44; *1774:* 47 (i); *1764:* 37 (i, abbreviated), 38; Horne *O;* Donath *A;* Lorengar *E*/Royal Opera Chorus and Orch/Solti

Decca SET443-4
London OSA1285

1980 (in Italian) *1764:* 1-38; Hamari *O;* Zempléni *A;* Kincses *E*/ Hungarian State Opera Chamber Chorus, Hungarian State Opera Orch/Lukács

Hungaroton SLPX12100-1

Index

142   *Index*